EMPTY LOGIC:
Mādhyamika Buddhism from Chinese Sources

EMPTY LOGIC:
Mādhyamika Buddhism
from Chinese Sources

by
Hsueh-li Cheng

PHILOSOPHICAL LIBRARY
NEW YORK

Library of Congress Cataloging in Publication Data

Cheng, Hsueh-li.
    Empty logic.

    Bibliography: p. 185
    Includes index.
    1. Mādhyamika (Buddhism) 2. Buddhism—China—
Doctrines.   I. Title.
BQ7457.C46   1983   181'.043'92   83-13246
ISBN 0-8022-2442-3

TO
THE MEMORY
OF
CHU HWANG-FANG
(1890-1941)

Contents

Preface

Recently many Westerners have studied Buddhist philosophy, especially the philosophical teachings of the Mādhyamika. Mādhyamika philosophy is considered to be "the most important outcome of Buddha's teaching"[1] and to represent "philosophical Buddhism par excellence."[2] The main message of Mādhyamika Buddhism is the doctrine of emptiness. Yet scholars as well as students of Buddhism have often been puzzled about this teaching and have misinterpreted it. The chief purpose of this book is to expound the Mādhyamika philosophy of emptiness as presented in Chinese sources and to clarify misconceptions about this important philosophy of Buddhism.

Mādhyamika Buddhism was founded by Nāgārjuna (*c.* 113-213) and introduced to China by Kumārajīva (344-413). This school of thought is known in China, Korea and Japan as the San-lun Tsung (Three Treatise School). It is also called the K'ung Tsung (the School of Emptiness). Its three main texts, namely, the *Middle Treatise* (*Chung-lun*), the *Twelve Gate Treatise* (*Shih-erh-men-lun*) and the *Hundred Treatise* (*Pai-lun*),[3] were translated into Chinese by Kumārajīva and his Chinese disciples more than two hundred years before Candrakīrti (600-650), the great Indian Mādhyamika, wrote the *Prasannapadā*. San-lun philosophy was well established in China by Seng-chao (374-414) and Chi-tsang (549-623) long before Indian Mādhyamika Buddhism was brought to Tibet in the eighth century. When contemporary Buddhist scholars discuss Mādhyamika Buddhism, they usually refer to the Sanskrit *Prasannapadā* or Tibetan sources in stating Nāgārjuna's philosophy. The present book is an attempt to present the earlier Chinese San-lun exposition of Nāgārjuna's thought.

Most contemporary Mādhyamika scholars regard the word *empty* or *emptiness* as a descriptive term referring to something, and the doctrine of emptiness as a metaphysical theory. Nāgārjuna is thought to argue for absolutism or nihilism. Actually, the word *empty* or *emptiness*, according to Chinese San-lun Buddhists, is not a descriptive term but a soteriological or tactical device. The doctrine of emptiness is not a metaphysical theory; rather it is essentially a way of salvation. This teaching is given not primarily to make a report about the world but to empty one of metaphysical speculation so that he can lose intellectual attachment.

Nāgārjuna investigated Buddhist as well as non-Buddhist metaphysical systems and rejected the metaphysical use of language. His critique of metaphysical views is often likened to Kantian or Wittgensteinian philosophy by contemporary scholars. In fact, Nāgārjuna's thought is quite different from Kant's and Wittgenstein's philosophies. He had his own unique teaching.

It seems to me that one of the most significant outcomes of Nāgārjuna's teaching was the creation of Zen (Ch'an) Buddhism in China. During the past few decades many Westerners have been fascinated by Zen teachings and practices. But few people know that Mādhyamika philosophy provides a major theoretical foundation for Zen as a "practical," "anti-intellectual," "irrational," "unconventional" and "dramatic" religious movement. In this book I will explore the influence of Mādhyamika thought upon Zen to help readers toward a better understanding of Zen Buddhism.

The book is divided into five chapters. Chapter one provides a general background of Buddhism to enable readers to perceive the place of Mādhyamika thought in Indian Buddhism and to know the development of the Mādhyamika movement in various parts of Asia. In chapter two, essential Mādhyamika doctrines are expounded. The chapter seeks to exhibit that the term *empty* or *emptiness*, which has no meaning by itself, obtains various meanings and uses in the process of salvation, and that the so-called middle way, the twofold truth and the refutation of erroneous views as the illumination of right views are just substitutes for emptiness. Chapter three examines the relation between Mādhyamika and Zen Buddhism and shows that central Mādhyamika doctrines have been assimilated into Zen teachings and practices. Chapter four is a presentation of the Mādhyamika approach to philosophical issues. It investigates how the Mādhyamikas treat the problems of reality, God and knowledge, why they refute metaphysical speculation and what their criticisms are with respect to certain philosophical viewpoints. Chapter five offers a brief comparison between Nāgārjuna's, Kant's and Wittgenstein's philosophies to suggest the unique nature of Nāgārjuna's teaching and explain why his philosophy cannot be identified with Kant or Wittgenstein. I describe why and how Nāgārjuna rejected conceptualization and argued for the emptiness of words.

The abbreviation *T* is given to represent the *Taishō Shinsū Daizōkyō* (the Taishō edition of the Chinese *Tripiṭaka*) throughout the book. There is a list of Chinese terms at the end, also a glossary which defines important Sanskrit, Pali, Chinese, Japanese and English words that are used. A selected bibliography is provided for those who want to know principal works on the main issues examined in this book.

I am indebted to a great number of persons who in one way or other have helped me in bringing this book to completion. To name them all would be impossible. But I wish to thank the late Dr. Richard Robinson, Dr. Minuro Kiyota and Dr. Martin Huntley for assisting me in the study of Mādhyamika thought. Thanks are due also to Dr. Timothy Woo, Dr. Kenneth K. Inada, Dr. Barry Curtis, Mr. John Paxson, Mrs. Jane Hoes, Miss Judy Graham and Mr. Marc Cohen who have helped by their valuable criticism of the early drafts of the manuscript. I am grateful to my former colleagues at Ohio University, Dr. Troy Organ and Dr. Gene Blocker, for their constant encouragement. The gentle advice of present colleagues at the University of Hawaii at Hilo, Dr. Evyn Adams, Dr. Donald Wells and the late Dr. Hideo Aoki, has greatly helped me in revising the manuscript. A special word of appreciation is also due to Dean David C. Purcell, Jr., who has offered secretarial assistance. I owe a debt of gratitude to the following publishers for permission to use certain passages: *Religious Studies*, Cambridge University Press; *Journal of Chinese Philosophy*, D. Reidel Publishing Company; Dialogue Publishing Company; *International Philosophical Quarterly*, Fordham University Press; *The Theosophist*, the Theosophical Society; D. Van Nostrand Company; University of Wisconsin Press; and Macmillan Publishing Co., Inc.

A special thanks is extended to the Chu Cultural Foundation for grants toward the publication of this book. The foundation was established in honor of Mr. Chu Hwang-fang, who was born at Ch'ao-chou, China, 1890 and went to *nirvāṇa* at Medan, Indonesia, 1941. Its chief goal is to promote the dharma of wisdom and brotherly love among mankind.

Finally and above all I want to express my deepest appreciation to my wife, Alice Chiong-huei Cheng, without whose loving support this work would not have been completed.

Chapter One

General Introduction

I. The Origin of Buddhism

Buddhism was founded by Śākyamuni,[1] whose personal name was Siddhārtha,[2] and family name Gautama, about 2,500 years ago. He was born in the village of Lumbini,[3] northern India, where his father was ruler of the Śākya clan. When young, Siddhārtha lived a luxurious life in his father's palace, but it is said that curiosity and a restless search for new pleasures led him to encounter the realities of life and sufferings of old age, sickness and death. These experiences invited him to quest for their solution.

Siddhārtha is alleged to have renounced his home at the age of twenty-nine and wandered the Ganges River Valley for six years. He studied traditional religious teachings with famous masters and joined some ascetics in their rigorous lifestyle, but his dissatisfaction continued. He then discounted traditional religions and their practices and went his own way. This eventuated in the moment which he later termed his enlightenment, and thenceforth he was known as the Buddha (the Enlightened One).

The Buddha spent the remaining forty-five years of his life

preaching his *Dharma*[4] (truth) and establishing the *Saṅgha*[5] (the Buddhist organization). He died at the age of eighty, having lived from approximately 563 B.C. to 483 B.C., which may be looked upon as the conjectural dates of the origin of the religious movement of Buddhism.[6]

The Buddhist religion was a reaction to traditional Indian Brāhmanism. It has occasionally been misinterpreted as something entirely new and different, yet it is a further growth of that ancient Indian religion and philosophy. The Buddha is reported to have said, "I have seen the ancient way, the Old Road that was taken by the formerly All-Awakened, and that is the path I follow."[7] Both Buddhism and Brāhmanism assert that our mundane existence is suffering and agree that ignorance and desire are the main sources of difficulty in life. They both claim that through right knowledge and good conduct we can secure release from the world of sorrow. In Buddhist as well as Brahman scriptures, the doctrine of karma is accepted. The present existence of an individual is, according to this doctrine, the effect of the past, and the future will be the effect of the present existence. All beings are born again and again in different spheres of life driven by their karmic forces.[8] Because of this belief, both Buddhists and Brahmans try to control karmic forces. They generally believe that liberation from the cycle of birth and death can only be attained after one develops certain physical and mental disciplines, such as meditation and other yogic practices, which often culminate in asceticism.

However, the Buddha disdained ritual and sacrifices, and his teaching was a protest against the over-elaborate ceremonialism of the traditional religion. He attacked the caste society of his time and refuted the inspiration and authority of the *Vedas*, the scriptures of orthodox Hinduism. He also repudiated the extreme ascetic life of traditional religious men and established the middle way. Perhaps the most important doctrinal difference between Buddhism and Brāhmanism is this: Brahmans assert the existence of *ātman* (I, self or ego), and consider the self as the innermost essence of man, essentially identical with *Brahman*, the supreme reality of the universe, but Buddhists deny the substantive view of the world and the soul,[9] and hold that everything in the universe, including the gods and the souls of all living beings, is in a constant state of flux.[10]

Hīnayāna and Mahāyāna Buddhism

After the death of the Buddha, Buddhism became popular and developed from early Buddhism into Hīnayāna (Small Vehicle) and then Mahāyāna (Great Vehicle) Buddhism.[11] The division between Hīnayāna and Mahāyāna Buddhism was established sometime between the first century B.C. and the first century A.D. Hīnayāna is the conservative Buddhist school which tries to preserve the orthodox teachings and practices of traditional Buddhism. It accepts the Pali canon as the main scriptures.[12] For Hīnayānists, there is only one Buddha, who is the founder of Buddhism, and the highest goal or level one can achieve in life is to become an *arhat*, a good disciple of the Buddha who attains salvation for himself by his own effort.[13]

Mahāyāna Buddhism is the later liberal Buddhist school which has a new interpretation of Buddhism. It does not accept the Pali canon as the sole scriptural source, but has many new scriptures written in Sanskrit.[14] According to Mahāyānists there is not just one Buddha, but many. In principle, everyone has buddha-nature and can become a buddha. The ideal one seeks to achieve is to become not merely an *arhat*, but a *bodhisattva*, a buddha-to-be, who has a great compassion for the world of mortals, and, after attaining salvation for himself, helps others to attain salvation.[15] The chief philosophical difference between Hīnayana and Mahāyāna is that while Hīnayānists assert the reality of *dharmas* (elements or entities), Mahāyānists declare that all things are empty.

Conservative Buddhism has been popular in Sri Lanka (Ceylon), Thailand, Burma, Cambodia and Laos. The people of these nations prefer the description Theravāda, which means "the system or school of the Elders,"[16] instead of Hīnayāna, which was given by the Mahāyāna. Mahāyāna Buddhism has been popular in China, Korea, Japan, Tibet, Mongolia, Nepal and Vietnam. Buddhism was the only religious and philosophical teaching of India to disseminate far beyond the borders of its homeland, and its spread north and east contributed to the development of other Eastern civilizations.

The Buddha as a Pragmatic Teacher

Modern scholars have differed in their reconstruction of the true or original teaching of the Buddha, but all seem to agree that the main issue the Buddha dealt with was how to expurgate suffering and evil from our lives. The aim of his teaching is to obtain *nirvāṇa* or salvation in a sorrowful world. He is said to have avoided the discussion of purely theoretical or metaphysical issues. When asked whether the world is eternal or non-eternal, whether finite or infinite, whether the soul is identical with the body and whether the saint exists after death, he maintained silence.[17] It seems that the answers to such metaphysical questions were, for the Buddha, intellectually uncertain, as illustrated in his famous parable of blind men describing an elephant. Metaphysicians can present only different partial views of metaphysical problems, like the conflicting one-sided accounts given by blind men who each touch only a part of the elephant.[18]

Many metaphysical questions were, according to the Buddha, inappropriate or even meaningless; they could not be answered by this or that, yes or no. His simile of fire explains why this is the case. Suppose someone asks, "In which direction has the fire which has run out of fuel gone—east or west, north or south?" This is really a senseless question because it assumes that fire is a separate entity which can exist without fuel. In fact there cannot be fire without fuel. Similarly, it is inappropriate or even meaningless to discuss whether the saint without any mark exists after death and whether the soul is identical with the body. These questions illegitimately assume that the soul is a separate entity, and that the saint without characteristics can be described as we describe an ordinary object with certain cognizable marks.[19]

When metaphysicians develop their theories, they are often bound by feelings, inclinations and pre-existing concepts. Their philosophical judgments are based on certain conscious or unconscious emotions and motivations rather than reasons and facts. They accept what they like, not what really is. No form of reasoning could make them see the truth. Buddha realized it was futile to establish a purely theoretical system to lead others to accept *dharma*. He is said to have stated: "How can men abandon their own views which they cherish as they organize them, led by inclinations and engrossed with their likes?... As they understand, so do they speak."[20]

Moreover, the examination of theoretical issues is counter-productive. A person who indulges in such speculation becomes all the more entangled in the net of theories he himself has woven. In fact, such a person, according to an analogy credited to the Buddha, acts like a foolish man wounded by a poisonous arrow. Instead of trying to dislodge the arrow, he wastes his time in speculation regarding the origin, nature and source of the arrow. Such a fool would die from infection before accepting medical treatment. The Buddha is described as a physician rather than a philosopher. He did not elucidate any purely theoretical issue, because, as he is reported to have said:

> this profits not, nor has to do with the fundamentals of religion, nor tends to aversion, absence of passion, cessation, quiescence, the supernatural faculties, supreme wisdom, and Nirvāna; therefore have I not elucidated it.[21]

The Buddha sought to enlighten people on the most urgent and important problems of misery, its origin, its cessation and the way leading to its cessation. He once said:

> And what...have I elucidated? Misery...have I elucidated; the origin of misery have I elucidated; the cessation of misery have I elucidated; the path leading to the cessation of misery have I elucidated. And why...have I elucidated this? Because...this does profit, has to do with the fundamentals of religion, and tends to aversion, absence of passion, cessation, quiescence, knowledge, supreme wisdom, and Nirvāna; therefore have I elucidated.[22]

The teachings of the Buddha are predominantly practical and pragmatic in character.

Philosophy in Early Scholastic Buddhism

Buddhism, however, did deal with certain philosophical problems and in Buddhism, religion and philosophy cannot be clearly separated. Unlike Christianity, Buddhism generally does not claim that one obtains salvation by faith, but holds that salvation is to be achieved by wisdom or true knowledge.[23] As stated in Buddha's teaching of the Four Noble Truths (misery, its origin, its cessation and the path leading to its cessation), ignorance is the origin of all evil and suffering, and true knowledge is the one and only reliable source of lasting liberation. The so-called true knowledge is the right understanding of the true nature of things. The Buddha is reported to have said: "So long as, monks, I did not thoroughly understand things as they really are...I did not declare myself to be truly enlightened, unsurpassed in the world with its devas, its Māras, its Brahmas, among the host of recluses and brahmins and of devas and men. But when, monks, I thoroughly understood them as they really are...then I declared myself to be truly enlightened, unsurpassed in the world with its devas, its Māras...."[24] Therefore Buddhists who hope to obtain salvation must pursue right knowledge by examining the reality of things. In light of this, knowledgeable Buddhists do spend much time in discussing philosophical issues by a predominantly intellectual approach.

The divisions or classifications of Buddhism are often due to different opinions or replies to metaphysical questions. Does there exist an external world? Is reality mental or physical or neither? And to epistemological questions: How do we know reality? Do we know reality directly or indirectly?

Vaibhāsika Buddhism,[25] a sect of Hīnayāna, asserts the reality of both physical objects and mind. The substance of things has a permanent existence throughout the three divisions of past, present and future. They argue that external objects are directly known by perception and not inferred. Our knowledge of external objects is no creation of subjective mind, but the discovery of objects presented to us. From this we know that external objects must exist because there cannot be perception without an object of perception. Thus the Vaibhāsikas come to hold a theory of dualistic direct realism.

Sautrāntika Buddhism,[26] another branch of Hīnayāna, also asserts the reality of both physical objects and mind, but claims that we do not have a direct perception of external objects. What we directly perceive are ideas, which are not the real objects but only copies. According to this school, the perception of external objects depends upon four factors: physical objects, subjective mind, sense and other auxiliary conditions. Whenever we perceive any external object, (1) there must be an object to give a certain form to consciousness, (2) there must be a mind to cause the consciousness of the form, (3) there must be a sense to determine what the consciousness is, and (4) there must be some auxiliary conditions such as light and position. All these factors combine to produce perception. If any one of them changes, we are bound to have a different perception. A good example is that things at a distance look smaller. Also objects are conceived differently by those with mental defects. Therefore the Sautrāntikas believe that the external world or objects have lost a part of their reality and become a hypotheti-cal cause of our images (*bāhyārtha-anumeyatva*). Our image or idea is a resemblance (*sārūpya*) between *viṣaya* (object) and *vijñāna* (mind).[27] By perceiving an idea, we can infer the exis-tence of an external object because there cannot be an idea without its cause.

The indirect realism of Sautrāntika theory is, in a sense, similar to John Locke's causal or representative theory of perception. According to Locke, we do not know things imme-diately but mediately, by means of ideas which are "whatever the mind perceives in itself, or is the immediate object of perception, thought or understanding."[28] Locke used the notion of causality to show that there are things which corres-pond to ideas. When we observe constantly recurring collec-tions of simple ideas, which are usually conveyed to us without our volition, we can infer that there are external objects which cause these ideas, at least during the time when the mind is passively receiving the ideas.[29]

The indirect realism of the Sautrāntika led to the idealism of the Yogācāra. The Yogācāra argue that if we know only our ideas and external objects are inferred, then only mind or ideas are real, and external objects are mental projections. This is quite similar to George Berkeley's idealism which came out of a criticism of Locke's representative theory of perception.

II. Mādhyamika in Indian Buddhist Thought

Buddhism in India developed in three main philosophical stages: (1) the early realistic and pluralistic system of the Hīnayāna, (2) the dialectical middle doctrine of the Mādhya-mika, and (3) the idealistic and monistic mind-only doctrine of the Yogācāra.

The first stage may embrace the early Buddhist thought of the Nikayas and the scholastic philosophy of the Abhidharmika. Although there are certain differences between the two systems,[30] they can both be regarded as realistic and pluralistic philosophies because they assert the reality or existence of something objective in the universe and that this reality (whether empirical facts or *dharmas*) is not just one but many. The Abhidharmika may include the Vaibhāsika and the Sautrāntika. The Vaibhāsika came into prominence in the third century after the Buddha's death, and the Sautrāntika in the fourth century after his death.

The Mādhyamika School was founded in the second century A.D. by Nāgārjuna, and the Yogācāra School in the fourth century A.D. by Asanga and his brother Vasubandu. The Mādhyamika is the central stage and also the turning point of Buddhism. Mādhyamika philosophy was a reaction against the direct and indirect realism of Hīnayāna philosophies as well as Brāhmanical systems, the Sāmkhya and the Nyaya-Vaiśesika.[31] The Mādhyamikas maintained that the teachings of the Buddha were not properly presented by any early Buddhist school. They came forth with a new interpretation of the Buddha's message and brought about a revolution in Buddhist thought. Epistemologically, Mādhyamika philosophy was a change from empiricism and dogmatism to dialectical criticism. In metaphysics, it argued for the rejection of metaphysical speculation. Religiously, it marked a change from a positivistic approach to a dialectical approach in the problem of the existence of God. Soteriologically speaking, the Mādhyamika produced a shift from the ideal of private egoistic salvation to the universal salvation of all beings. Mādhyamika teachings changed the picture of the Buddha's philosophy and laid the foundation for the establishment of Yogācāra philosophy. Subsequently they represented a landmark in the history of Indian philosophy.[32]

Mādhyamika and Early Scholastic Buddhism

Unlike early scholastic Buddhists who made an ontological

commitment to a certain reality, the Mādhyamikas claimed that they did not hold any view of their own and that the purpose of their teachings was to examine critically all metaphysical views and refute them by exposing absurdities or contradictions. According to the Mādhyamikas, any speculation about the true nature of things is erroneous and should be rejected. For them, it is dogmatic for the Brāhmanical philosophers to hold that the reality of the universe is one *ātman*, and it is also dogmatic for the Abhidharmika Buddhists to contend that the reality of the universe is many *dharmas*.[33]

For the Mādhyamikas, the early scholastic Buddhist concept of *dharmas* is contradictory to, or at least incompatible with, the Buddha's teaching that all things are causally interdependent and hence are empty.[34] The early scholastic Buddhists, so claimed the Mādhyamikas, had an improper understanding of the Buddha's teaching. When the Buddha talked about the doctrine of *anātman*, he did not mean the doctrine of *dharmas* to be an ultimate tenet. For him, *rūpa*, *vedanā* and other *dharmas* were as illusory as *ātman*. The true meaning of his teaching is the doctrine of *Śūnyatā*: All things are empty. Emptiness here means in part that all things are devoid of definite nature, characteristic and function. It also means that speculative theories are unintelligible and should be refuted.

The Mādhyamikas developed a new approach to the problem of the existence of God. According to them, it is wrong to say that God exists, and it is also wrong to say that God does not exist. God is as empty as *ātman* and *dharmas*; the concept of God as the creator or maker of the universe is unintelligible. In the *Twelve Gate Treatise*, Nāgārjuna presented several arguments to show that so-called creation, making, production or origination cannot be established and thereby demonstrated that the terms *creator*, *maker*, *producer* and *originator* are not genuine names referring to reality. Accordingly, it is nonsensical to assert God's existence as the creator or maker of the world.[35]

The Mādhyamika criticism of the concept of God differs from the early scholastic Buddhist denial of God's existence. The scholastic aimed at leading people to accept that *dharmas* are the only reality. For Mādhyamikas, the so-called *dharmas* are as empty as God. *God* is an unintelligible concept not because it denotes no *dharma*, but rather because the concept leads to certain absurdities or contradictions. From the standpoint of Mādhyamika philosophy, early scholastic Buddhist atheism was a new dogmatic metaphysics since it made an ontological commitment to something; hence it was to be ruled out.

The Mādhyamika doctrine of emptiness brought about a change from the ideal of personal salvation to that of the universal salvation of all beings. Since all things are empty, nothing, according to the Mādhyamikas, has a determinate and self-abiding nature or character which cannot be changed. In principle, all men can be converted to Buddhism and enter into *nirvāṇa*. Their teaching of emptiness encourages everyone to transcend himself and thereby attain transcendental wisdom. It also posits the potential to obtain perfect freedom and unconditional liberation from attachment, desire and ignorance. Salvation is not just for the select but for all, and one can help another in gaining enlightenment. The goal of salvation is not merely to become an *arhat*, a venerable person who obtains his salvation through effort, but a *bodhisattva*, an enlightened being who postpones his entrance into *nirvāṇa* for the purpose of helping other creatures, and eventually becomes a *Buddha*, a man of perfect freedom.

However revolutionary it may be, Mādhyamika thought is not an entirely new viewpoint but can be traced to the original teaching of the Buddha who called his teaching the middle (*madhyamā*) way and refuted extreme doctrines. Actually, Hīnayānists also referred to the middle way. Early Buddhist literature tells us that there were four main pairs of extremes the Buddha would have liked to refute.[36]

The Mādhyamikas adopted the middle way approach and attempted to maintain a mean between extreme affirmation and extreme negation, and to establish the doctrine of *Śūnyatā*. This doctrine was stated by early Buddhists[37] and had been well developed by Buddhists before Nāgārjuna, as is observed in the *Prajñāpāramita Sūtras*. Its ideal is *niṣprapañca*, the inexpressible in speech and unrealizable in thought. The main message of *Prajñāpāramitā* literature[38] is that all things are empty and supreme enlightenment is identified with the attainment of *Śūnyatā*. The object of the religious discipline of Buddhism is to find, in this realization, an unattached abode referred to as *apratiṣṭhita* (not abiding). The genuinely enlightened being has no dwelling place in the sense that his thoughts and doings have no external objects in view to which he desires to adapt himself, and hence he is "like the sun shining on everybody just and unjust, or like the lily blooming in its best even when there is nobody around to admire its supra-Solomonic array."[39] The *Prajñāpāramita* philosopher says, "A *Bodhisattva-Mahāsattva* should abide himself in the perfection of *Prajña* by abiding in emptiness.... The *Tathāgata* (a title of the Buddha) is so called because he is not abiding anywhere, his mind has no abode neither in things created nor in things uncreated, and yet it is not away from them."[40] Nāgārjuna developed his teachings under the influence of *Prajñāpāramita* philosophy.[41] Later his philosophy paved the way for the development of Mahāyāna Buddhism not only in India but also in China, Japan, Tibet and other parts of Asia.

Mādhyamika and Yogācāra

The Yogācāra accepted most of the Mādhyamika criticism of the early realistic and pluralistic philosophy of the Abhidharmika and also denied the reality of the object. They too advocated the doctrine of *Śūnyatā* and the middle way, and held that reality "can neither be called existence nor nonexistence. It is neither 'such' nor 'otherwise.' It is neither born nor destroyed. It neither increases nor decreases. It is neither purity nor filth. Such is the real '*lakshana*' [mark] of the transcendental truth."[42]

Although Mādhyamika exercised enormous influence upon later Mahāyāna Buddhists, it failed to convince many to discontinue using concepts and entities to describe and explain the origin and nature of things. It seems that these Buddhists had some good reasons, and they presented effective ways of refuting Mādhyamika. One of the most popular and efficient arguments used by the Yogācāra to criticize Mādhyamika was this: every object, both mental and non-mental, may be logically or dialectically proven illusory. But in order to be illusory, there must be a certain thought which suffers from illusion. The very fact of illusion itself proves the existence and reality of a certain consciousness or mind. To say that everything mental and non-mental is unreal is intellectually suicidal. The reality of something should at least be admitted in order to make sense of talking about illusion. To the Yogācāra, Mādhyamika appeared an unwarranted extremism.

The Yogācāra modified the concept of *Śūnyatā*. While the Mādhyamika consider all things to be *śūnya* or void, the Yogācāra argue that *śūnya* or void of characteristics must designate something. For *śūnya* to be a justifiable term, we must assume the existence of that which is void. If not, how can there be a void? We may falsely perceive a rope as a snake and elephants in a dream. There is no *rūpa* (matter or form) outside the thought, yet with all these imaginary things there must be something, some substratum, and this substratum, according to the Yogācāra, is *vijñāna* (mind or consciousness). The Yogācāra are supporters of *Vijñanavāda* (idealism). They deny the real existence of all except *vijñāna* and assert that all things in the universe are merely the manifestation of mind.[43]

The Yogācāra maintained the middle way doctrine but developed it by refuting and harmonizing what they thought to be the extreme views of the Abhidharmika and Mādhyamika. It is wrong, so the Yogācāra stated, for the Abhidharmika to assert the existence of both mental and non-mental. Following the Mādhyamika, they attacked the Abhidharmika and denied the reality of material objects. On the other hand, they claimed that the Mādhyamika denial of the existence of both mental and non-mental is also erroneous. They, like the Abhidharmika, accepted the reality of the mind. According to the Yogācāra, *all is real* and *all is unreal* are both incorrect forms of *Śūnyatā*. The formula should be: that which appears is real, not the manner of its appearance. The rope is devoid of the snake appearance, but it is not devoid of its nature as a rope. For this school, (1) the form of an appearance, the duality of subject and object, is unreal, but (2) that which appears, the substratum, *vijñāna*, is real. The first point attacks Abhidharmika realism; the second point disagrees with Mādhyamika philosophy. The Yogācāra identified *śūnya* with mind or consciousness to avoid both the dogmatism of realism (acceptance of the reality of external objects and mind) and the scepticism of dialectical negation (rejection of the reality of external objects and mind).

According to this Yogācāra idealism, all thoughts except those of a buddha have a threefold character or nature: (1) the imaged character (*parkialpita*), (2) the dependent or caused character (*paratantra*) and (3) the ultimate or transcendental character (*pariniṣpanna*). Unlike the Mādhyamika, the Yogācāra did not consider all phenomena merely void, but divided them into those which have an image character and those which have dependent or caused character. The first do not exist and hence are void, but the second do exist and are temporarily real. When we perceive the rope as a snake, the snake does not exist but the rope does. The Yogācāra maintained that behind the phenomenal world there is a noumenal, ultimate reality; this is mind or consciousness. It is not the ordinary psychological mind but Suchness, *Tathatā*, Buddhahood or mind stripped of everything transient and phenomenal. "This is the transcendental essence of everything," said Vasubandu, "and it is termed 'Suchness' because its essential nature is real and eternal. But the real nature of Suchness is beyond the reach of human language; it is indefinable."[44] In the strict sense, the reality of the universe is beyond differentiation and verbal description, and we cannot ask whether it is universal or particular. So like the Mādhyamika, the Yogācāra rejected pluralism and asserted monism.

In Yogācāra Buddhism the classification of knowledge is based on metaphysical conclusions; its epistemology is related to its metaphysics. Corresponding to the threefold character or nature of being, there are, according to the Yogācāra, three forms of knowledge. This threefold division of knowledge in fact developed out of the Mādhyamika teaching of twofold truth. The Yogācāra seem to divide the Mādhyamika's relative or worldly truth in two: the *parikalpita* (illusive) and the *paratantra* (relative). Illusive knowledge is an incorrect judgment which proceeds from wrongly comprehending the nature and relationship of objects. It is a purely subjective elaboration that is unverifiable. Many of life's troubles are due to this illusory aspect. Suppose a man steps on a rope in the dark and, imagining it to be a snake, is frightened. This is *parikalpita*, a wrong judgment or imaginative construction attended with unwarranted excitement.

However, not all knowledge of the phenomenal is illusory. We have another form of knowledge, the knowledge of experience, which is *paratantra*. The characteristic feature of this knowledge is that it is not altogether a subjective creation produced by imagination, but a construction of some objective reality on which it depends for material. It is due to this knowledge that all kinds of objects, external and internal, are recognized, and in them individuality and generality are distinguished. Suppose the man who steps on the rope in the dark bends down, examines it closely, and finds it to be a piece of rope. This then is relative knowledge. It is empirical, pragmatic and useful in daily life. Most philosophical and religious teachings belong to this category. They benefit the unenlightened.

Hence, unlike the Mādhyamika, the Yogācāra make a distinction between relative and illusory knowledge of what we perceive, which seems to correspond to the distinction between that which appears (the rope) and the manner of its appearance (the snake). Relative knowledge has at least a certain degree of truth, but illusive knowledge is an intellectual mistake, and some affective functions are set in motion along with the wrong judgment. The Yogācāra could criticize the Madhyamika for failing to make this distinction.

However, like the Mādhyamika, the Yogācāra hold that there is absolute or ultimate knowledge which does not belong to demonstrative knowledge or sensuous experience. Both schools of thought agree that the doctrine of *Śūnyatā* cannot be understood by ordinary reasoning. Absolute truth is available only when we reach the state of self-realization by going beyond appearance and relativity. In such a state the rope is perceived in its true perspective. From the absolute point of view, the rope is a reflection of mind and has no objectivity apart from the mind or consciousness. This is real knowledge of the rope. Unless one goes beyond the realm of relativity and experiences what lies behind the world of the rope, no true knowledge is possible. Absolute knowledge is for the enlightened, *is* the enlightenment which leads to salvation.

Thus from the Yogācāra's standpoint, everything possesses *parikalpita*, *paratantra* and *parinispanna*. Ontologically, each being or thing has an imaged, dependent and transcendental character; and, epistemologically, from each being or thing we may receive illusive, relative and transcendental knowledge. If we perceive a rope as a snake, we see the imaged character of the rope and have illusive knowledge. If we know the rope as a piece of a rope, we see the dependent character of the rope and have relative knowledge. Both imaged and dependent characters belong to the phenomenal world, and our knowledge of them cannot be unconditionally true. However, if we understand the rope as mind or consciousness, we see its transcendental nature and have the absolute truth.

III. The Development of Mādhyamika Buddhism

Nāgārjuna's teaching was well developed by his eminent disciple, Āryadeva (c. 163-263 A.D.). Like his master, Āryadeva was also born in South India. He wrote many books to expound Nāgārjuna's thought. Owing to his propagation, Mādhyamika teaching became popular among non-Buddhists as well as Buddhists. In India the school split into two sects, the Prāsangika and the Svātantrika, sometime after the fifth century. The Prāsangika insisted that Nāgārjuna did not hold any view but merely exercised *prasanga (reductio ad absurdum)* to refute all views. Candrakīrti was the champion of this Mādhyamika school.

The Svātantrika contended that the Mādhyamika can and should hold a positive view. Some Svātantrikas accepted the philosophical teachings of earlier Indian Sautrāntika Buddhism, and others those of Yogācāra Buddhism. So Svātantrika Mādhyamika divided into two groups, the Sautrāntika Svātantrika and the Yogācāra Svātantrika. The latter was brought to Tibet in the eighth century. It is known as the Dhu-ma-pa and continues to exist today. But Mādhyamika Buddhism seemed to decline in India around the eleventh century and to disappear after the fifteenth century.

In China Mādhyamika Buddhism is called the San-lun Tsung (Three Treatise School) because it is based upon three main texts: (1) Nāgārjuna's *Middle Treatise* with commentary by Piṅgala in 445 verses, (2) his *Twelve Gate Treatise* translated from the now lost *Dvādāsa-dvāra-śāstra*, including verses and commentary by Nāgārjuna,[45] and (3) the *Hundred Treatise* with main verses by Āryadeva and commentary by Vasu.

Kumārajīva was the initial teacher of Mādhyamika Buddhism in China. He came to China about 401 A.D. and converted many Chinese to Buddhism. Some of his disciples, such as Hui-yüan (334-416), Seng-jui (352-446) and Seng-chao (374-414), used Taoist and Confucian terms to expound Mādhyamika Buddhism so that Mādhyamika teaching could be understood by Chinese, and consequently Mādhyamika thought flourished among Chinese intellectuals during six dynasties. However, the spread of the San-lun School in China after Kumārajīva was also due to the efforts of Seng-lang (494-512), Seng-chüan (d. 528), Fa-lang (507-581) and especially Chi-tsang (549-623). Perhaps Chi-tsang was the greatest San-lun master in the history of San-lun Buddhism in China, Korea and Japan. Besides his famous commentaries on the *Middle Treatise*, the *Twelve Gate Treatise* and the *Hundred Treatise*, Chi-tsang wrote many other important San-lun works such as the *Profound Meaning of Three Treatises* and the *Meaning of the Twofold Truth*. With Chi-tsang, San-lun philosophy was well established in China.

San-lun Buddhism as a sectarian school began to decline after Chi-tsang died. And when the Yogācāra (Fa-hsiang School) was introduced to China by Hsüan-tsang (600-664), the Mādhyamika as a sectarian school began to disappear. Yet Sam-non-jong (the Korean pronunciation of Chinese San-lun Tsung) continued in Korea until the fifteenth century. This Buddhist school of thought is called the Sanron Shū (Three Treatise School) in Japan. From Prince Shōtoku's time (574-622) to the Nara period (708-781), it was one of the major Buddhist schools in Japan, yet never existed as an entirely independent sect or institution. However, it has been required as an academic discipline. Today most non-Buddhist as well as Buddhist colleges in Japan offer courses in the study of Mādhyamika Buddhism.

In brief, Mādhyamika Buddhism was founded by Nāgārjuna in the second century. Subsequently it spread in India from the second to the fourteenth centuries, in China from the early fifth to the eighth or ninth centuries, in Korea from the sixth to the fifteenth centuries, in Japan from the seventh to the mid-twelfth centuries, and in Tibet from eighth century until today.

Outline of Mādhyamika Movement

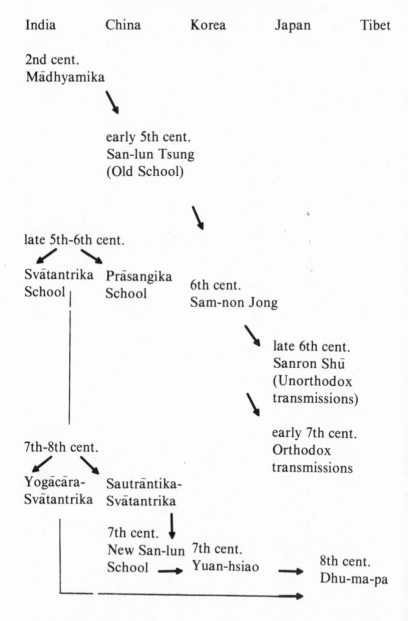

India   China   Korea   Japan   Tibet

2nd cent.
Mādhyamika

early 5th cent.
San-lun Tsung
(Old School)

late 5th-6th cent.

Svātantrika   Prāsangika
School   School   6th cent.
                              Sam-non Jong

                                    late 6th cent.
                                    Sanron Shū
                                    (Unorthodox
                                    transmissions)

                                    early 7th cent.
                                    Orthodox
7th-8th cent.   transmissions

Yogācāra-   Sautrāntika-
Svātantrika Svātantrika

             7th cent.
             New San-lun   7th cent.
             School   →   Yuan-hsiao   →   8th cent.
                                           Dhu-ma-pa

Chapter Two

Principle Mādhyamika Doctrines

The main teachings of Mādhyamika Buddhism focus on emptiness (*k'ung*), the middle way (*chung-tao*), the twofold truth (*erh-t'i*) and the refutation of erroneous views as the illumination of right views (*p'o-hsieh-hsien-cheng*). These doctrines are interrelated and aim at showing that all things are empty.

The word *empty* or *emptiness*, for the Mādhyamika, has no meaning by itself but acquires a meaning in the process of salvation or *nirvāṇa*. The Mādhyamika doctrine of emptiness is not a metaphysical theory; it is primarily a soteriological device for purifying the mind so that one may be empty of emotional and intellectual attachment to objects of desire and knowledge. This doctrine is believed to be the central message of Buddhism and was first expressed as the doctrine of the middle way in the Buddha's First Sermon.[1] The middle way is essentially a way of emptiness; it is a path demonstrating that speculative reasoning is unintelligible and that one should not be attached to a view. In Mādhyamika teaching, emptiness and the middle way are often interchangeable. The San-lun Tsung in China, Korea and Japan is known as the K'ung Tsung (the School of Emptiness) or the Chung-tao Tsung (the School of the Middle Way).

The Mādhyamika doctrine of the twofold truth is considered a summary of Nāgārjuna's treatment of truth, knowledge and wisdom. The twofold truth has often been conceived by Mādhyamika scholars as referring to two fixed sets of truth[2] and standing for two realities,[3] and the term *emptiness* is regarded as denoting a certain ineffable absolute essence beyond ordinary manifestation.[4] However, Chinese San-lun texts indicate that Nāgārjuna's twofold truth neither refers to two fixed sets of truth nor stands for two realities. It is merely a pedagogic device (*chiao-t'i*) used to illumine the Buddha's message so that sentient beings can be free of ignorance and illusion. The doctrine of twofold truth is really a way of emptiness, a means of knowing the empty nature of truth, knowledge and wisdom so as to remove intellectual attachment.

The middle way and twofold truth are convenient means to assist people to eliminate erroneous views and thus to empty the mind. In this respect they serve as substitutes for emptiness while one is in the process of purging oneself of delusion and passion. According to Chinese San-lun masters, the refutation of erroneous views is the illumination of right views; it is not necessary to present other views but simply to discard false views. The more wrong views one refutes, the closer one is to liberation. In other words, the absence of wrong views is itself the right view. Therefore, to say that all things are empty is not to argue for a new metaphysics. Once this is realized, one can discover that even truth should be discarded.

I. The Middle Way

Buddha's Teaching of the Middle Way

The name *Mādhyamika* was derived from the Sanskrit noun *madhyamā*, meaning middle or neutral. Mādhyamika philosophy was called so because it proclaimed the doctrine of the middle way by refuting extremist epistemological, metaphysical and religious views of Brāhmanism, Hīnayāna and other Mahāyāna Buddhist schools. According to the Mādhyamika, the doctrine is the original teaching of the Buddha. After he obtained enlightenment, the Buddha preached the doctrine of the middle way to five mendicants. He is said to have taught them:

> Devoting oneself to ascetic practices with an exhausted body only makes one's mind more confused. It produces not even a worldly knowledge, not to speak of transcending the senses. It is like trying to light a lamp with water; there is no chance of dispelling the darkness....

> To indulge in pleasures also is not right; this merely increases one's foolishness, which obstructs the light of wisdom....[5]

He then summarized the experience of his life: "I stand above these two extremes, though my heart is kept in the Middle. Sufferings in me have come to an end; having been freed of errors and defilements, I have now attained peace."[6]

Buddha's teaching of the middle way is primarily concerned with a way of life that one ought to follow. He advised the five mendicants not to live a pessimistic ascetic life nor to live a hedonistic, worldly life, but to go above the two extremes because only then could they attain peace.

Nāgārjuna's Middle Way of Eightfold Negation

Nāgārjuna accepted the Buddha's doctrine of the middle way and extended it to deal not only with the problem of a way of life but also with all philosophical and religious issues.[7] He found that philosophers and religious men often had a dualistic way of thinking; they tended to describe events as appearing or disappearing, permanent or impermanent, similar or dissimilar, and arriving or departing. For the Mādhyamikas, such descriptions were extreme. They asserted that the middle way doctrine of the Buddha advised the avoidance of extremes in order that a person might become free from the concepts of *is* and *is not*. The middle way rises above affirmation and negation. It is a path for removing dualistic thinking. Nāgārjuna opened the *Middle Treatise* with these words:

> I salute the Buddha,
> The foremost of all teachers,[8]
> He has taught
> The doctrine of dependent co-arising,[9]
> The cessation of all conceptual games.[10]
> No origination, no extinction;
> No permanence, no impermanence;
> No identity, no difference;
> No arrival, no departure.[11]

Mādhyamika eightfold negation is a convenient term for the negations of origination, extinction, permanence, impermanence, identity, difference, arrival and departure. There are eight negations because Nāgārjuna selected and refuted eight characteristics which were then commonly considered essential to any event. Actually the thrust is a wholesale negation of attempts to characterize things.[12]

The Mādhyamika Dialectic

Mādhyamika eightfold negation is undertaken by means of a dialectic in the form of *reductio ad absurdum*.[13] Nāgārjuna analyzed traditional Buddhist and non-Buddhist theories which attempted to describe the nature of reality and displayed that each theory led to contradictions or absurdities. He used the principles of reasoning used by his opponents to lead them to see that their theories involved contradiction. If the concept or conceptual system led to contradiction, it could not depict reality because freedom from contradiction is accepted as a necessary condition of truth.

Mādhyamika dialectic is not intended to establish a thesis but merely to expose the absurdity or contradiction implied in an opponent's argument. It is purely analytic in nature until there is no position left to be proved. The Mādhyamika is said not to have his own logic. The contradictory or absurd consequences revealed by the dialectic are unintelligible in light of the opponent's logic only.[14] The main logical apparatus by which Nāgārjuna criticized all views is the tetralemma (*ssu-chü*). This argumentative device assumes that there are four possible views: (1) affirmation, (2) negation, (3) both affirmation and negation, and (4) neither affirmation nor negation. Nāgārjuna used the tetralemma to examine the opponent's philosophy and show that anything as being, as non-being, as both being and non-being, or as neither being nor non-being, is untenable and should be ruled out. This way of refutation is well illustrated in his analysis of causality.

Nāgārjuna's dialectic method is a type of conceptual analysis; it purports to show that all the concepts or categories through which we construct experience are unintelligible. For example, the concept of production cannot be explained; its nature is incomprehensible. In the *Twelve Gate Treatise*, Nāgārjuna wrote that a careful analysis of the process of production reveals that it consists of: (a) the part which is already produced, (b) the part which is yet to be produced and (c) the part which is being produced. But (a) is finished, (b) is not yet and (c) can be established if and only if (a) and (b) are established. Hence, the act of producing is impossible. If there is no act of production, then there cannot be a producer, so the process or act of producing and the producer are both unreal. Like production, other concepts or categories involve contradictions or absurdities. Nāgārjuna advised, "If conceptualizations are permitted there will arise many, as well as great, errors."[15] "Covetousness, enmity, and delusion are said to arise from false ideation or conceptualization."[16]

The middle way is a negation of conceptualization, according to the Mādhyamika, because subjectively the mind is deluded with illusion, ignorance and prejudice, and objectively characterization or description must involve contradiction or absurdity.

The Middle Way as Emptiness

In his *Middle Treatise* Nāgārjuna wrote, "For the sake of removing all kinds of erroneous views, the Buddha teaches *Śūnyatā*."[17] Nāgārjuna's interpretation of this doctrine claims that the true nature of an object cannot be ascertained by intellect and described as real or unreal, mental or non-mental.

That which is real, he asserted, must have a nature of its own (*svabhāva*) and should not be produced by causes or depend on anything else. To say that a certain being or becoming is real, would contradict the fact that phenomena are bound by the relations of cause and effect, subject and object, actor and action, whole and part, unity and diversity, duration and destruction, and the relations of time and space. Anything known through experience is dependent on conditions, so it cannot be real. According to the Mādhyamika, the perceived object, the perceiving subject and knowledge are mutually interdependent. The reality of one is dependent upon others; if one is false, the others must be false. When a rope is perceived as a snake, the perceived object, the snake, is false. The perceiving subject and knowledge of the external object must also be false. So what one perceives within or without is illusory. Therefore there is nothing, neither mental nor non-mental, which is real. On the other hand, what one perceived cannot be conceived as unreal since that which is unreal can never come to exist. Thus a thing cannot be said to be either real or unreal, and accordingly any such claim would be unintelligible.

In Nāgārjuna's thought, the middle way as emptiness is often presented as a provisionary name for the fact that all things are causally dependent upon each other, the classic Buddhist doctrine of dependent origination or causality (*pratītyasamut-*

pāda).[18] He often used *pratītyasamutpāda* to refute extreme views and to prove the emptiness of all things. In his teaching, emptiness, the middle way and dependent origination are interchangeable,[19] and lead to the conclusion that metaphysical theories are untenable.

In the strict sense, emptiness, the middle way and dependent origination, according to the Mādhyamika, are themselves empty. Still, they are good devices for helping rid people of attachment. They perform the same function of avoiding the extremes of absolutism and nihilism. The claim that all things are empty means that all things neither absolutely exist nor absolutely do not exist. If things in the universe existed absolutely, they would have their own nature and would not be dependent upon causal conditions, but nothing in the world is seen to be independent of causal conditions. Thus the existence of things cannot be absolutely real. And if the existence of things were absolutely unreal or nothing, there would be no change or motion in the universe, yet myriad things are perceived to arise from causal conditions. So the absolutist and the nihilist notions of existence and non-existence are unacceptable. This topic was well treated by the Chinese Mādhyamika Seng-chao: "If you would say that they exist, their existence arises non-absolutely. If you would say that they do not exist, their forms have taken shape. Since they have forms and shapes, they cannot be the same as the non-existent. So, this explains the idea of the emptiness of the non-absolute."[20]

The middle way and *pratītyasamutpāda* are two ways of designating the same notion, namely, emptiness. Both aim at showing that the true state of things is incomprehensible and indescribable, beyond the reach of thought and language.[21] Things appear to exist, yet when one attempts to understand the real state of their existence the intellect is baffled. Therefore things should be declared inexplicable, and conceptualization and speculative reasoning abandoned.

II. The Twofold Truth

Saṁvṛtisatya and Paramārthasatya

According to the Mādhyamika, one should understand the doctrine of *Śūnyatā* by means of the twofold truth, namely the conventional or relative truth (*saṁvṛtisatya*, *su-t'i*) and the ultimate or absolute truth (*paramārthasatya*, *chen-t'i*). Nāgārjuna said: "All Buddhas taught *Dharma* by means of the twofold truth for the sake of sentient beings. They taught by means of, first, the conventional truth, and second, the ultimate truth."[22]

Nāgārjuna's idea of the twofold truth reflects a difference in the manner in which one may perceive things and the point of view from which one looks at them. Worldly or conventional truth involves emotional and intellectual attachment to what one perceives, and hence objects of knowledge are considered fixed, determinate and self-existing. When one sees things from this standpoint, he is committed to linguistic conventions as well as ontological entities. The meaning of a word is believed to be the object for which the word stands. The true nature of things can be described and explained by language. This standpoint is *saṁvṛtisatya*, often presented as discursive knowledge.[23]

However, one may see what he perceives from a different point of view, namely, the standpoint of transcendental or ultimate truth whereby he re-evaluates the phenomenal world without attachment. One can know that things perceived are empty of a fixed, determinate or self-existing nature. From this standpoint, one is committed neither to ontological entities nor linguistic ideas. The meanings of words are seen as human projections. Language cannot give true nature and conceptualization is abandoned. This unattached standpoint is *paramārthasatya*.[24] Nāgārjuna wrote, "Those who are unaware of the distinction between these two truths are incapable of grasping the profound meaning of the Buddha's teaching."[25]

Saṁvṛtisatya is for ordinary unenlightened people. In the strict sense it is ignorance (*avidyā*). It does not give the real nature of things but distorts it. To be enlightened one should go beyond conventional truth and come to *paramārthasatya*. This is to eliminate attachment and ignorance, and see things through the eyes of wisdom (*prajñā*) instead of worldly eyes.

A Tactical Device

The twofold truth is essentially a tactical device. According to Chi-tsang, this device has been established to defend Buddhism against possible charges of nihilism and absolutism, to help sentient beings know Buddha's *Dharma* and to explain certain obscurities and inconsistencies in the teachings of the Buddha.[26]

It seems that the issue of whether Mādhyamika philosophy is nihilism or not was anticipated by Nāgārjuna himself. He explicitly warned that *Śūnyatā* should not be considered non-being, nothingness or non-existence.[27] His doctrine of the two-fold truth is designed chiefly to clear away this misconception. Yet many contemporary scholars, including H. Kern, Max Walleser, La Vallée Poussin and A.B. Keith, have held that Mādhyamika philosophy is nihilism or negativism. H. Kern said that Mādhyamika thought is "complete and pure nihilism."[28] A.B. Keith wrote, "In the Mādhyamika...the absolute truth is negativism or a doctrine of vacuity,"[29] and argued that for Nāgārjuna the universe is "absolute nothing."[30] Recently Harsh Narain reaffirmed this interpretation of the Mādhyamika: "[Mādhyamika philosophy] is absolute nihilism rather than a form of absolutism or Absolutistic monism."[31]

For Nāgārjuna, those who see *Śūnyatā* as nothingness or non-existence fail to know the profound significance of the distinction between worldly and transcendental truths. They assume that there is only one universal standpoint from which to examine all things, while actually the Buddha's teachings were presented by means of the twofold truth. That is, the doctrine of emptiness should be examined from two standpoints, worldly truth and transcendental truth.

Nāgārjuna acknowledged that from the standpoint of worldly truth, objects appear as if they had an existence independent of the perceiver. The truth classifies objects as chair, table, I, mind or other sensible things, and in this manner is used to carry on everyday affairs. What Nāgārjuna wanted to deny is that empirical phenomena, causally interdependent, are absolutely real. From the transcendental standpoint all things are devoid of fixed, determinate and self-existing essence. However, to say that nothing is absolutely real does not mean that nothing exists. It does not nullify anything in the world. It does not deny the universe but avoids making an essential differentiation and metaphysical speculation about it. This does not imply that his philosophy is nihilism.

In answer to an opponent who charged that Śūnyavāda is nihilism and makes Buddhism impossible, Nāgārjuna said, "Really you don't understand the nature, purpose and meaning of Śūnyatā. Hence you have frustration and confusion."[32] He argued that to refute the doctrine of Śūnyavāda and insist that all things have fixed and determinate essence or substance, would make Buddhism impossible. If the essence of all things were fixed and determinate, there would be no such phenomena as change, origination and destruction, and hence there would be no suffering. Since there would be no noble truth of suffering, there could be no noble truths of the origin of suffering, the cessation of suffering and the way leading to the cessation of suffering. If there were no Four Noble Truths, there would be no four fruits of śramaṇa.[33] Without the four fruits there would be no goal for religious life and realization of the Saṅgha would not be possible. "Without the noble truths the true Dharma would not exist. Without the Dharma and Saṅgha, how could there be the Buddha?"[34] Thus the Three

Jewels of Buddhism, Buddha, Dharma and *Saṅgha*, would be denied.

Further, if all things are not empty and have determinate nature, "anyone who is not a Buddha in virtue of his own nature cannot hope to attain enlightenment even by otherwise serious endeavor or by the practice of the *Bodhisattva* way."[35] *Nirvāṇa* would be impossible. It is only when *Śūnyatā* prevails that Buddhism is possible. Evil men can become good, and the unenlightened can attain nirvāṇa. Hence Nāgārjuna claimed: "With *Śūnyatā*, all is possible; without it, all is impossible."[36] Thus the doctrine of emptiness is given to save, or to account for, empirical phenomena and practical affairs.

Nāgārjuna's twofold truth has also been considered as two fixed sets of truth. His distinction between *saṁvṛtisatya* and *paramārthasatya* has been taken to imply or correspond to an ontological distinction between "relative reality" and "absolute reality." For numerous other scholars emptiness, viewed from the standpoint of ultimate truth, must stand for an absolute essence or reality, and Mādhyamika thought would be called absolutism. For example, T.R.V. Murti recently wrote: "I have interpreted *śūnyatā* and the doctrine of Two Truths as a kind of Absolutism, not nihilism."[37]

Actually, Mādhyamika philosophy is not absolutism. For Nāgārjuna, all concepts, including the term *Śūnyatā*, are incomplete symbols or provisionary names. They do not stand for entities and of themselves have no meaning. As he remarked, "If there is a thing that is not empty, then there must be something that is empty. Since nothing is non-empty, how can there be an empty thing?"[38] To emphasize that emptiness is not primarily an ontological concept and does not refer to any absolute reality, he warned that "in order to refute all erroneous views, the Victorious One teaches emptiness. He who holds that there is an emptiness will be called incurable by all Buddhas."[39]

Like emptiness, the twofold truth is a tactical device. The

bodhisattva, who seeks to help himself and others obtain enlightenment, has wisdom and knows that conventional truth depends upon words and names that, from an ultimate stance, should be eliminated. However, because he has compassion to help ignorant beings who have only discursive knowledge, and because the preaching and exposition of Buddhism must depend on words and concepts, the *bodhisattva* cannot be silent. How can he both be silent and have unattached *prajñā*, and show compassion at the same time? For Nāgārjuna, this can be done by means of the twofold truth.

Worldly truth, though not unconditional, is essential for the attainment of the ultimate truth and *nirvāṇa*; according to Nāgārjuna's *Middle Treatise*, "without worldly truth, ultimate truth cannot be obtained."[40] Relative truth is not useless in achieving enlightenment, nor can it be said that there is no relation between worldly and ultimate truths. Transcendental truth is explained by speech, and speech is conventional and conditional. The *bodhisattva* knows and practices this teaching of the twofold truth. He uses words and concepts, but realizes that they neither stand for, nor point to, anything substantial. He employs *pratītyasamutpāda* to refute extreme views, and recognizes that they are all empty. It is this skill-in-means (*fang-pien*) which enables him to live in conditional and transcendental worlds simultaneously, and hence to save and benefit himself and others equally. The *Twelve Gate Treatise* states: "If one does not know two truths, he cannot know self-interest, other-interest and common-interest. But, if one knows conventional truth, he then knows ultimate truth; and if he knows ultimate truth, he knows conventional truth."[41]

The Mādhyamika doctrine of the twofold truth has also served as an exegetical technique; it is used to explain contradictions in Buddhism and make the Buddha's teachings "all true."[42] There do seem to be ambiguities and even contradictions in expressions of Buddhist *Dharma*. For example, Buddhist texts sometimes state that all things are causally produced and impermanent, but at other times state that causal production and impermanence cannot be established. The scripture may contrast enlightenment (*vidyā*) with ignorance (*avidyā*), yet say that dualistic thinking should be rejected. Which of these teachings is true?

The Buddha was a practical teacher and his teachings were given according to the intellectual and spiritual condition of his audience. Different messages were delivered from different standpoints, and each has to be known from its appropriate standpoint. No truth is true by itself but is recognized as true in a context. So-called conventional and ultimate truths designate two main contexts or standpoints. All Buddhas presented their teachings by means of these truths. From the conventional stance they may claim that things are causally produced and impermanent, and contrast enlightenment with ignorance. As far as conventional truth is concerned, these teachings are true. Yet Buddhas may regard things from a transcendental stance and say that causal production and impermanence cannot be established, and that dualistic thinking should be rejected. One who tries to understand Buddhist teachings should examine them by means of the twofold truth. In doing so, he will find that there are no contradictions and that all Buddha's *Dharma* is true.

The Emptiness of the Twofold Truth

The two truths, according to Chi-tsang in his *Meaning of the Twofold Truth*, are not exhaustive of all truths, nor are they two fixed sets of truth.[43] If the higher truth is considered to stand for a determinate or self-existing essence, or one clings to it as something absolute, it becomes lower, ordinary truth.[44] Ultimately, no truth for Chi-tsang is "absolutely true."[45] All are essentially pragmatic in character and eventually have to be abandoned.[46] Whether they are true or not depends on whether they lead one to clinging or non-clinging. Their truth-value is their effectiveness as a means (*upāya*) to salvation. The twofold truth is like medicine.[47] In order to refute the annihilationist the Buddha may say that existence is real, and for the sake of rejecting the eternalist he may claim that existence is unreal.[48] As long as the Buddha's teachings are able to help remove attachment, they can be accepted as true.[49]

Like the middle way, the twofold truth is essentially a way of emptiness, a path eliminating extreme views.[50] After extremes and attachment are banished from the mind, the so-called truths are no longer needed and hence are not truths anymore.[51] One should be empty of all truths and lean on nothing.

III. The Refutation of Erroneous Views as the Illumination of Right Views

Illumination through Negation

To understand the doctrine of emptiness one should know, according to Chi-tsang's *Profound Meaning of Three Treatises*, that "the refutation of erroneous views is the illumination of the right view" (*p'o-hsieh-hsien-cheng*). The Mādhyamikas examined all views. Their refutation of erroneous views is, in philosophical context, a declaration that metaphysical views are erroneous and should be refuted. For the Mādhyamikas, the refutation of false views and the illumination of right views are not two separate acts but the same. A right view is not a view in itself, rather the absence of views. If a right view is held in place of an erroneous one, the right view itself will become one-sided and require refutation. A main message of Nāgārjuna's teaching of emptiness, expressed in contemporary terms, is that one should refute all metaphysical views, and to do so does not require the presentation of another metaphysical view, but simply abolishing all metaphysics.

The metaphysical speculation of things is often critically examined in the Buddhist scriptures. When the scripture denies that a *dharma* exists, it does not imply that the text holds another view that a *dharma* does not exist. For the Mādhyamika, the metaphysical speculation of non-existence is as untenable as that of existence. If anyone holds that a *dharma* does not exist, this would be another extreme view to be rejected. The term *does not exist, non-being* or *non-existence* is employed in the Buddhist scriptures, yet one should know, according to Chi-tsang, that "the idea of non-existence is brought out primarily to handle the disease of the concept of existence. If that disease disappears, the useless medicine is also discarded."[52] To negate both existence and non-existence, in the strict sense, is not to affirm or negate anything because all things are empty. Chi-tsang wrote, "Originally there was nothing to affirm and there is not now anything to negate."[53]

Two Kinds of Negation

In explaining that the refutation of erroneous views neither entails nor implies that one has another view, the Mādhyamika made a distinction between negation for affirmation and pure negation. They questioned the thesis that negation must negate something and argued for pure negation. In one case, negation is used with the aim of affirmation, establishing another thesis: *Not-p* implies something other than *p*. The judgment "The apple is not black" is based upon another judgment, "The apple is red." But for Nāgārjuna, negation is used merely to affirm negation itself. *Not-p* means only the absence of *p*. There is no affirmation implied. The purpose of Mādhyamika refutation is simply to expose self-contradiction or absurdity without making any commitment whatever.[54]

According to the Mādhyamika, language is like a game, and our debate whether x is y or x is not y is like a magical creation. Suppose there are two men both created by magic. One does a certain thing and the other tries to prevent him from doing it. In this case the action and the prevention are equally illusory, yet it makes sense to say that one prevents the other. Similarly, according to Nāgārjuna, his own words are empty, like things created by magic or illusion, and yet he can refute the essence of all *dharmas*. His negation is not a negation of something real. Nāgārjuna argued: "Just as a magically formed phantom could deny a phantom created by its own magic, so could negation and refutation."[55]

Certain contemporary scholars have held that Mādhyamika negation is similar to the *neti, neti* (not this, not that) expression in the ancient Upaniṣads[56] and that Mādhyamika Buddhist thought is the same as Upaniṣadic absolutism. For instance, S. Radhakrishnan has stated: "All negation depends on a hidden affirmation....Nāgārjuna admits the existence of a higher reality, though with the Upaniṣads he considers it to be not an object of experience."[57] D.T. Suzuki held a similar viewpoint: "Nāgārjuna's famous doctrine of 'The Middle Path of Eight No's' breathes the same (Upaniṣadic) spirit (Absolute Reality is to be described by No, No!)."[58]

But perhaps Nāgārjuna's negation is quite different from Upaniṣadic negation. The latter assumes the existence of an inexpressible essential substratum, and the main aim of its negation is to describe, by negation, an absolute which cannot be expressed. The Mādhyamika negations do not assume an inexpressible essential substratum, nor is their purpose to describe, by negation, this reality, rather to deny that there can be such a reality. It would therefore seem inappropriate to identify Mādhyamika philosophy with Upaniṣadic absolutism.[59]

Emptiness of Right and Wrong

Nāgārjuna's negation is only a tool for eliminating extreme views. If there is no extreme to be removed, there need be no such things as affirmation and negation. Words such as *right* and *wrong* or *erroneous* are really empty terms without reference to entities or things. The right view is actually as empty as the wrong view. To Chi-tsang's understanding, it is cited as right "only when there is neither affirmation nor negation,"[60] and if possible one should not use the term. But "we are forced to use the word 'right' (*ch'iang-ming-cheng*) in order to put an end to wrong. Once wrong has been ended, then right no longer remains. Then the mind is attached to nothing."[61]

The Mādhyamika refutation of erroneous views and illumination of right views is a therapeutic device for abolishing intellectual and emotional attachment. To obtain enlightenment, one has to go beyond right and wrong, true and false, and see the empty nature.

IV. Emptiness

A Soteriological Device

For the Mādhyamikas, the Buddha was not a speculative metaphysician but a practical soteriologist at heart. His chief concern was the salvation or *nirvāṇa* of sentient beings from the sorrowful world. In teaching men to achieve *nirvāṇa*, the Buddha was believed to be a skillful teacher. On the one hand, he knew that all words and concepts are empty, and that discursive reasonings should be avoided. But on the other hand, he understood that sentient beings are attached to mundane things and could know only discursive knowledge. In order to help them free from various attachments, he employed words such as the middle way and extreme views, worldly and ultimate truths, illumination and negation, and emptiness and non-emptiness, to expound his *Dharma*. Actually "the true nature of all *dharmas* is entirely inexplicable and unrealizable."[62] Thus all doctrines or verbal messages the Buddha gave are nothing but skillful means (*upāya*) used to achieve the goal of non-attachment.

Still men tend to be attached. This clinging or longing is likened by the Mādhyamika to a disease or fire, a source of suffering, delusion and ignorance in life. Emptiness is a soteriological device to expunge the disease or fire so that human beings are released from misery and so it is likened to medicine or water. The Mādhyamikas have argued that one should properly understand the nature, purpose and function of the device, and not be bound to it. Otherwise, one cannot be transformed. "If water could extinguish fire," Chi-tsang expressed it, "and then again produce fire, what would we use to extinguish it? The view that things come to an end or are eternal is the fire, and emptiness can extinguish it. But if one still clings to emptiness, then there is no medicine that can eliminate the disease."63

The Middle Way of Twofold Truth as a Way of Emptiness

For the Mādhyamikas, the tetralemma, the logical apparatus by which they show each view leads to contradiction or absurdity, is also a convenient means. Its four expressions are not exhaustive of alternatives. The Mādhyamikas often took more than four alternative views on certain subjects. They also examined views from two different standpoints, namely the standpoints of worldly and of ultimate truth. This dialectical method has been called the middle way of the twofold truth (erh-t'i-chung-tao). It can be seen in Chi-tsang's twofold truth on three levels (san-tsung-erh-t'i or erh-t'i-san-kuan).64

(1) On the first level, ordinary people hold that what appears to the senses is the true nature of things. They accept the reality of things and think that *dharmas* are real and possess being. But saints and sages know that *dharmas* are empty in nature, and reject the commonsense view of the universe. The first is regarded as worldly truth and the second as ultimate truth.

(2) The second level explains that both being and non-being belong to worldly truth, whereas non-duality (neither being nor non-being) belongs to ultimate truth. This is to say that both the worldly and ultimate truths of the first level, when viewed from a higher standpoint, can be ascribed only to the sphere of worldly truth because the affirmations of being and non-being are extreme. Similarly, the affirmations of permanence, and impermanence, and of *nirvāṇa* and the cycle of

life-and-death, are extreme. The middle way is to refute these extremes, and hence non-duality (neither permanence nor impermanence, and neither the cycle of life-and-death nor *nirvāna*) is the ultimate truth.

(3) On the third level, both duality and non-duality are worldly truth, whereas neither duality nor non-duality is ultimate truth. The two truths of the previous level are extremes from the standpoint of this level because duality is pluralistic while non-duality is monistic. Pluralism is an extreme and monism is also an extreme. As two extremes, they are therefore called worldly truth. Only that which is neither pluralistic nor monistic can be regarded as the middle way or ultimate truth.

Chi-tsang's levels may be said to represent degrees of spiritual maturity. The advance from one level to another is the process of salvation or transcending the world. The doctrines of the middle way of eightfold negation, emptiness, and a distinction between worldly and ultimate truths can be comprehended from different levels. An understanding of their meaning depends on the degree of one's spiritual maturity and the aspect of reality which has come into view.

The Mādhyamika dialectical process is a means of purifying the mind, not limited to three levels but to be employed progressively to infinite levels until one is free from conceptual attachment. No matter how far one proceeds, if the mind is or tends to be devoted to something or some view, the dialectical process will need to be exercised repeatedly until every tinge of delusion is removed. In *The Profound Meaning of Three Treatises* Chi-tsang wrote:

> Mahāyāna truth is beyond all predication. It is neither one nor many, neither permanent nor impermanent. In other words, it is above all forms of differentiation or, as its adherents might say, it transcends both difference and identity. In order to make this clear, San-lun doctrine teaches that each thesis that may be proposed concerning the nature

of truth must be negated by its antithesis, the whole process advancing step by step until total negation has been achieved ...until everything that may be predicated about truth has been negated.[65]

Various Meanings of Emptiness

The word *emptiness* or *empty* gains its true connotations in the process of salvation or *nirvāṇa* and has different meanings during the process. All things may be empty in the sense that they are devoid of definite nature, characteristic or function. Emptiness may be used to discredit theories and dismiss viewpoints. To claim that all things are empty may show that discursive reasonings and conceptual statements about the true nature of things are unacceptable. The term is also used to devalue and to designate things worthless, useless, to be discarded. To empty one's mind may mean that one sees the world as suffering and transcends it.

Various meanings of emptiness are exemplified in the successive stages of Mādhyamika negation. On the first level, emptiness means that commonsense things, which appear to be real, are not really real. Chi-tsang expressed this as the denial of being. But emptiness in this sense may be misinterpreted as non-being or nothing. People distinguish between being and non-being, existence and non-existence, permanence and impermanence, *saṁsāra* (the cycle of life and death) and *nirvāṇa*. All these are *svabhāvically* construed[66] (the attached way of thinking) and should be regarded as extremes.

On the second level, emptiness is employed to revoke dualistic thinking. The term *empty* means that both naive realism and nihilism are unintelligible and their descriptions of the world should be discarded. Here the doctrine of emptiness is expressed as the denial of both being and non-being. However, at this stage one may still be attached to conceptualization and to a monistic view of the universe.

Because any conceptualization is an extreme, on the third

level emptiness implies that monistic as well as dualistic and pluralistic views of the world are untenable. It is the negation of conceptualization, stated as a denial of both duality and non-duality. At this stage, one is supposed to be free from all attachments. If this occurs, emptiness means non-attachment.

It should be noted that to obtain liberation one need not pass through three levels or even infinite stages of a gradual progression; one can achieve enlightenment instantly. Emptiness is like a medicine: one may take medicine many times before the disease is cured while others may take it just once. Also, no matter how one gets enlightenment, when attachment is gone, emptiness should be discarded.[67] To realize this "non-abiding" nature of emptiness is true wisdom. This is the achievement of *mokṣa* (salvation).[68]

In summary, the term *empty* or *emptiness* is mainly a soteriological device, a tool of *nirvāṇa*. Psychologically, emptiness is detachment. The teaching of emptiness is to empty the mind of cravings. Morally, this negation has a positive effect, namely, preventing one from doing evils and making one love oneself and others. It is to foster the virtue of compassion (*karuṇā*). The ideal of life is the *bidhisattva* rather than the *arhat*. Epistemologically, emptiness is an unattached insight that truths are not absolutely true. It teaches that discursive knowledge does not provide true wisdom and that enlightenment is the abandonment of conceptual thinking. Metaphysically, emptiness means that all things are devoid of definite nature, characterisic and function, and that metaphysical views are unintelligible and should be discarded. This is not to advocate nihilism but rather to save or to account for the possibility of empirical phenomena and practical values. Spiritually, emptiness is freedom or liberation from the suffering of the world.[69]

Chapter Three

Mādhyamika and Zen

Zen Buddhism often appears to be anti-intellectual, illogical and trivial. These apparent aspects of Zen have puzzled many students of Buddhism. Why is Zen so irrational? By what Buddhist doctrine, tenets or philosophy did Zen masters develop their unconventional and dramatic teachings and practices? It seems that the principle San-lun Mādhyamika doctrines—emptiness, the middle way, the twofold truth and the refutation of erroneous views as the illumination of right views—have been absorbed into Zen teachings and practices. Mādhyamika thought offers a major theoretical foundation for Zen as a practical, anti-intellectual, irrational, unconventional and dramatic religious movement.

Scholars who are familiar with Zen Buddhism know that Zen was influenced by Taoism and Yogācāra Buddhism, yet few realize that Chinese San-lun Buddhists made great contributions to the formation and development of Zen. Those who discuss the influence of Mādhyamika Buddhism upon Zen have not given it the sufficient and adequate attention it merits. They often assume that the Mādhyamika Śūnyatā has a definite meaning by itself and stands for absolute reality, and that Mādhyamika dialectical negation affirms this reality, and they hold that Zen is the application of this teaching.[1] Mādhyamika

55

Buddhism is said to have led to "Illogical Zen."[2] But as we have seen, the word *empty* has for the Mādhyamika no meaning of itself and Mādhyamika negation is not intended to affirm, nor is Zen so irrational as is ordinarily supposed. San-lun Mādhyamika thought can help us clear away certain absurdities, contradictions or inconsistencies in Zen teachings and practices.

The main Mādhyamika texts, the *Middle Treatise*, *Twelve Gate Treatise* and *Hundred Treatise*, had been translated into Chinese and were well known among Chinese Buddhists more than a hundred years before Bodhidharma (470-543), the First Patriarch of Chinese Zen Buddhism, went to China in 520. Hui-neng (638-713) is regarded as the real founder of Zen Buddhism, although he was the Sixth Patriarch. He lived more than a hundred years after Chi-tsang, who developed and systematized Chinese San-lun Mādhyamika philosophy. A study of Mādhyamika teachings had been an academic discipline of Buddhist monks in China and Japan since the sixth century. Nāgārjuna was in fact regarded as the venerable patriarch by Zen Buddhists. Both Bodhidharma and Hui-neng, and also their followers, must have known San-lun works and accepted Mādhyamika teachings. In fact, Zen masters such as Niu-t'ou Fa-yung (594-657) and Nan-ch'uan P'u-yuan (748-834) were San-lun Buddhists before they became Zen masters.

A comparative study of San-lun and Zen literatures shows that although Mādhyamika philosophy appears to be logically argumentative and Zen does not, they have many parallel doctrines. The main San-lun Mādhyamika tenets have been assimilated into Zen Buddhism, and in many respects Zen appears to be a practical application of Mādhyamika thought.

I. Zen and Emptiness

Many Zen writings and stories indicate that Zen Buddhism accepted the doctrine of *Śūnyatā*. This can be seen in the following conversation reported between Bodhidharma and the Emperor Wu-ti (502-549):

The Emperor:	"Since my enthronement, I have built many monasteries, copied many holy writings and invested many priests and nuns. How great is the merit due to me?"
Bodhidharma:	"No merit at all."
The Emperor:	"What is the Noble Truth in its highest sense?"
Bodhidharma:	"It is empty, no nobility whatsoever."
The Emperor:	"Who is it then that is facing me?"
Bodhidharma:	"I do not know, Sire."[3]

The ultimate and holiest principle of Buddhism, according to Bodhidharma, is the doctrine of emptiness. It means that all things, including merits, nobility, a knower and knowing, are empty. It is said that Hung-jen, the Fifth Patriarch residing at Yellow Plum in Chin-chou, made an announcement that anyone who could prove his thorough understanding of Buddhism would be given the patriarchal robe and proclaimed his successor. Hui-neng is said to have inherited the robe by composing this poem:

There is no Bodhi-tree,
Nor stand of a mirror bright.
Since all is void,
Where can the dust alight?[4]

This poem suggests that the teaching of emptiness is the essence of Zen Buddhism. It states not only that evils, passions and physical objects are empty, but also that enlightenment and the religious training to get rid of delusions are empty. Although Zen was influenced by Yogācāra idealism and claimed that the mind is the Buddha,[5] the so-called mind, for

certain Zen Buddhists, is really empty. The Zen teaching of the
emptiness of mind is well illustrated in the following conversation between Tao-kwang, a Yogācāra Buddhist, and a Zen
master:

Tao-kwang:	"With what frame of mind should one discipline oneself in the truth?"
Zen master:	"There is no mind to be framed, nor is there any truth in which to be disciplined."
Tao-kwang:	"If there is no mind to be framed and no truth in which to be disciplined, why do you have a daily gathering of monks who are studying Zen and disciplining themselves in the truth?"
Zen master:	"I have not an inch of space to spare, and where could I have a gathering of monks? I have no tongue, how would it be possible for me to advise others to come to me?"
Tao-kwang:	"How can you tell me a lie like that to my face?"
Zen master:	"When I have no tongue to advise others, is it possible for me to tell a lie?"
Tao-kwang:	"I cannot follow your reasoning."
Zen master:	"Neither do I understand myself."[6]

As we have seen, one of the most important meanings of
emptiness in Mādhyamika Buddhism is the negation of conceptualization. Zen has seemed to accept this teaching and
subsequently rejected any conceptual way of thinking. Like the
Mādhyamikas, Zen Buddhists have claimed that men are
slaves to concepts, and that enlightenment is liberation from
conceptual thought. The intellect appears a useful tool to find
truths but may be the worst enemy of religious experience.

Tsung Kao, a Zen master, said that "conceptualization is a deadly hindrance to the Zen yogis, more injurious than poisonous snakes or fierce beasts.... Brilliant and intellectual persons always abide in the cave of conceptualization; they can never get away from it in all their activities. As months and years pass they become more deeply engulfed in it. Unknowingly the mind and conceptualization gradually become of a piece."[7] Anyone who wants to obtain salvation should eliminate conceptualizations.[8]

The negation of conceptualization, for the Mādhyamika, means no-thought and no-abiding. Sixth Patriarch Hui-neng and his followers seem to follow this model and "set up non-thought as the main doctrine, non-form as the substance, and non-abiding as the basis.... No-thought is not to think even when one involves in thought. Non-abiding is the original nature of man."[9] To achieve no-thought and non-abiding is to realize that the true nature of things is unintelligible and incomprehensible, and not to use any verbal and written statements to depict reality.

Like the Mādhyamikas, Zen Buddhists use the word *empty* not as a descriptive name but as a convenient device to purify one's mind. Tao-chien asked the master Fa-yen: "Does the Void contain the six phenomena?" The master responded: "Void." Tao-chien was immediately awakened. After he had made a bow to express his heartfelt gratitude, the master asked him, "How did you become enlightened?" Tao-chien answered: "Void."[10] The word *empty* or *void* here performs the function of stopping further intellectual pursuit, thus awakening the devotee.

The Zen acceptance of *Śūnyatā* as the negation of intellectual speculation and as a soteriological device for purifying one's mind seems to have led Zen Buddhists to develop a non-speculative approach to attaining enlightenment. It has also led them to emphasize practical rather than purely theoretical aspects of Buddhist religion. When men discover that the intellect cannot give true wisdom, they tend to pursue a non-intellectual way of obtaining salvation and are practical, not theoretical, in dealing with religious problems. Chinese San-lun masters often considered Nāgārjuna as a man of meditation (*dhyāna*) rather than intellect, so it is not surprising that Nāgārjuna was later accepted as a patriarch by Zen Buddhists. This seems one source of Zen Buddhists' preference for practical meditation over conceptual understanding of Buddha's *Dharma* and one reason why their teachings appear irrational and even anti-intellectual.

Many or even most Buddhists deify the Buddha and mythologize his teachings. They think of him as supramundane, transcendent, and give him a special ontological status. For such, the term *Buddha* or *Tathāgata* denotes an absolute essence or deity who is both ultimate reality and a loving person.[11] Mādhyamikas considered this a mispresentation of Buddha's teaching, and their doctrine of emptiness denies an ontological commitment to anything, even the Buddha. They explained away all the theological speculation of Buddhism as erroneous or extreme views.[12] Again, their teaching seems to have exercised an influence upon Zen. Certain Zen Buddhists neither deify the Buddha nor offer him any special ontological status. For instance, when Gautama Buddha was born, he is said to have proclaimed, "Above the heavens and below the heavens, I alone am the Honored One!" Zen master Yün-men (d. 966) commented on this story by saying, "If I had been with him at the moment of his uttering this, I would surely have struck him dead with one blow and thrown the corpse into the maw of a hungry dog."[13] Other Zen Buddhists have spoken of him as nothing more than "a stick of dry dung"[14] or "three pounds of flax."[15] "When you meet the Buddha, kill the Buddha; when you meet the Patriarch, kill the Patriarch."[16]

Zen masters follow the Mādhyamika in not allowing themselves to become attached even to the Buddha and Buddhism. It would seem that a major difference between Mādhyamika and Zen is that the former uses logical tools and presents arguments to show that speculative theories are unintelligible and should be discarded, while Zen Buddhists do not engage in arguments but simply accept the conclusion of Mādhyamika reasonings and put it into practice.

II. Zen and the Middle Way

According to the Mādhyamikas, the reason for rejection of speculative theory is not merely that subjectively one's mind may be deluded by concepts, but also that objectively all conceptual thought is dualistic and leads to contradictions or absurdities. To avoid erroneous views, one should adopt the middle way and eschew the *is* and *is not*. It seems very likely that under the influence of this Mādhyamika teaching of the middle way, Zen Buddhists too have rejected dualistic thought.

Actually, Zen Buddhists have paraphrased Mādhyamika statements on this subject. For instance, Hui-neng made the following statement to deny the concepts of *is* and *is not*:

The true nature of an event is marked by
No permanence, no impermanence;
No arrival, no departure;
No exterior, no interior;
No origination, no extinction.[17]

His denial of these dichotomous ideas as essential marks of anything is almost identical with Nāgārjuna's statement of the middle way of eightfold negation. They are similar not only in meaning but also in choice of words.

Like Mādhyamika eightfold negation, Zen negation is not merely eight negations but a wholesale negation of all views. Zen Buddhists undertook more than eight negations;[18] the process does not stop until intellectual and emotional attachments are expunged from the mind. For Zen as well as the Mādhyamika, the middle way is a tool to help people not to be attached to anything, including emptiness. Fa-yung said: "Do not abide in the extremity of the Void, but illumine the non-being in the being. It is neither out of the Void nor out of being. Void and being are not conceived of as two. This is called the Middle Way."[19]

According to the Mādhyamikas, verbal statements are a dualistic expression and involve contradictions or absurdities, yet the Buddha made verbal statements in order to help sentient beings know his message and gain enlightenment. So what is, by Mādhyamika lights, really contradictory or absurd can function as a beneficial means, and the Mādhyamika doctrine of the middle way is supposed to show this paradoxical nature of techniques used by the Buddha. This may have inspired or justified Zen masters when they employed inconsistent, senseless, trivial or ridiculous statements to display their understanding of Buddhism or to awaken disciples to Zen. For example, when Tung-shan (807-869) asked Pen-chi (840-901), "What is your name, monk?" the terse reply was "Pen-chi." Tung-shan said: "Say something more." The response was, "I won't." Tung-shan persevered, "Why not?" The answer was, "My name is not Pen-chi."[20]

A monk asked Chao-chou (778-896), "All things return to oneness. Whither does oneness return?" Chao-chou replied: "When I was staying at Chin-chou, I made a robe of cloth weighing seven pounds."[21] How illogical Pen-chi's statements are and how odd Chao-chou's answer! They seem to be out of reason. But Zen literature abounds with such irrationalities.

This approach may puzzle and even shock many students of Buddhism, but for Zen, as well as for Mādhyamika, all instructions and techniques are empty. The so-called logical or rational statements, when viewed from a higher standpoint, are really as absurd or contradictory as those statements which appear to be illogical or irrational. The former can be useful, why not the latter? After all, they are all merely convenient means to help people to gain enlightenment, and eventually have to be declared useless and be discarded. Actually, to make a clear-cut distinction between logical and illogical, rational and irrational, is dualistic and should be ruled out. Here resides the explanation for Zen's seemingly illogical and irrational appearance.

Zen Buddhists do not hold extreme or determinate positions; there is no definite method or instruction for them to follow. The great Zen teachers seldom stuck to fixed patterns in expressing themselves and often exhausted every possible means, including unconventional shouting, kicking, beating and keeping silent, to enlighten people. Their religious experiences seem to suggest that enlightenment can be achieved in many different ways, even without formal education or conventional religious discipline.[22] Since all things are equally empty, any incident can be a right occasion for awakening if one's mind is ripened for the moment. One can have *satori* (*wu*, enlightenment) listening to a senseless remark, hearing an inchoate voice, seeing a tree grow or experiencing a trivial event such as drinking tea, opening a door or reading a book. The practice of Zen embodies the conclusion of Mādhyamika Buddhism although the premises have never been stated. It assumes the Mādhyamika claim that all things are devoid of definite nature, character and function, and advises that anyone can be awakened by any event in any situation and is free to use any style to discuss truth and employ any way to attain salvation. In these respects again, Zen is a practical application of Mādhyamika thought.

III. Zen and the Twofold Truth

According to the Madhyamika, their teaching should be understood by means of the twofold truth, a convenient term for the standpoints of worldly and ultimate truths. The former sees things from a point of view deluded with ignorance, illusion and prejudice, while the latter sees things from a point of view that transcends. This teaching seems to have been assimilated into Zen Buddhism. Zen masters often expressed themselves through the twofold truth; their messages and practices are supposed to be understood from two standpoints. Seen in this light, many "paradoxical words and strange acts" (*chi-yen chi-hsing*) do not appear so unintelligible as one might at first believe. Examine the following cases:

(1) A monk asked the Sixth Patriarch: "Who has attained to the secrets of Huang-mei (Yellow Plum, the name of the mountain where the Patriarch used to reside)?"

The Sixth Patriarch replied: "One who understands Buddhism has attained to the secrets of Huang-mei."

The monk asked: "Have you then attained them?"

The master answered: "No, I have not."

The monk wondered: "How is it that you have not?"

The master said: "I do not understand Buddhism."

(2) The Sixth Patriarch beat Shen-hui with a stick and asked: "Do you feel a pain?"

Shen-hui answered: "I am both painful and painless."

(3) The master said: "I have a thing which has neither head nor tail, neither name nor word, and neither back nor face. Does anyone know what it is?"

Shen-hui stated: "That is the essence of the Buddha, my Buddhahood."[23]

Since Hui-neng was Sixth Patriarch, he should have known Buddhism and attained to the secrets of Huang-mei; otherwise, why would the Fifth Patriarch have appointed him his successor? However, when viewed from the higher standpoint, all things, including Buddhism and the secrets of Huang-mei, are empty. Thus Hui-neng stated that he did not understand Buddhism. When we are beaten, we usually feel pain, yet this pain is really empty. Therefore, Shen-hui expressed the twofold truth by saying, "I am both painful and painless." The common belief is that whatever can be conceived to exist must have characteristics or marks such as a head, tail, back, face or name. Yet all things when examined from the higher point of view are "empty and without characteristics" (*chen-k'ung wu-hsiang*). Hui-neng's and Shen-hui's utterances in case (3) were made from this position. Thus one cannot comprehend Zen without understanding the doctrine of the twofold truth.

Many Zen paradoxes are actually the practical applications of the Mādhyamika doctrine of the twofold truth. The aim of these applications is to awaken people. As long as they can help people to get enlightenment, their verbal expressions, no matter how they are asserted, can be accepted as "true." Truth, according to Zen and Mādhyamika, is pragmatic in character and the truth of such utterances consists in their effectiveness as a means to realizing *nirvāṇa*.

Like the Mādhyamika, Zen Buddhists hold that the twofold truth does not stand for two fixed sets of truth but represents degrees of spiritual maturity. Some may achieve enlightenment instantly, but others may take several steps. Zen Buddhists seem to use the Mādhyamika idea of the middle way of twofold truth or the twofold truth on three levels to explain stages of spiritual growth. This can be seen in a famous statement given by Ch'ing-yuan (d. 740):

Before I had studied Zen for thirty years, I saw mountains as mountains, and waters as waters. When I arrived at a more intimate knowledge, I came to the point where I saw that mountains are not mountains, and waters are not waters. But now that I have got its very substance I am at rest. For it is just that I see mountains once again as mountains, and waters once again as waters.[24]

Like Chi-tsang, Ch'ing-yuan has divided the process of enlightenment into three levels. At first, naively, mountains are just mountains. But this naive view should be refuted: in reality mountains are not simply mountains, the true state of things cannot be identified with sense appearances. Yet this negation may lead to the denial that there are mountains or waters at all, construed as nihilism or scepticism. The perspective of the middle way rejects these extremes and from a higher point of view sees the same things without delusion: in this sense mountains are once again mountains and waters once again waters.

According to the Mādhyamikas, the scale of enlightenment is not limited to three levels; it is possible and even auspicious if one can see that all things are empty only by knowing that one thing is empty. The opening statement in most chapters of Nāgārjuna's *Twelve Gate Treatise* is to this effect: "All things are empty. Why? Because something, x, is empty."[25] Most chapters of the treatise end with these sentences: "Since x is empty, all created things are empty. Since created things are empty, all non-created things are empty. Since created and non-created things are empty, what of the self?"[26] Certain Zen Buddhists, too, hold that one may have to go through more than three levels to realize the empty nature,[27] but also believe that one can achieve enlightenment abruptly. It is characteristic of the Hui-neng school of Zen that *satori* (*wu*) comes upon one instantly. If the emptiness of a tiny thing is known, the emptiness of all things will be understood.[28]

Actually, since all things are empty, according to Zen Buddhists one may not have to practice anything at all, not even to obtain truth and enlightenment. It is said that Shen-hui once asked the Sixth Patriarch, "Through what practice should one work that one may not fall into a 'category'?" The Sixth Patriarch replied, "What have you been doing?" Shen-hui answered, "I do not even practice the Holy Truth!" "In that case, to what category do you belong?" "Even the Holy Truth does not exist, so how can there be any category?"[29] Thus, like the Mādhyamikas, Zen Buddhists hold that truths are merely convenient means, also empty and eventually to be discarded.

Ultimately, no truth-claim should be made and no word should be spoken. Chao-chou (778-897) asked Master Nan-ch'uan (748-834), "Please tell me what it is that goes beyond the four alternatives and the hundredfold negations." Na-ch'uan made no answer but went to his room.[30] Yang-shan (814-890) asked Master Kuei-shan (771-853), "When the great action is taking place, how do you determine it?" Master Kuei-shan immediately came down from his seat and went to his chamber. Yang-shan followed him and entered the room. Kuei-shan said to him, "What was it you asked me?" Yang-shan repeated the question. Kuei-shan said, "Don't you remember my answer?" Yang-shan replied, "Yes, I remember it." Kuei-shan then pressed him further. "Try to say it to me." Yang-shan immediately left the room.[31]

Such stories seem to show that for Zen, ultimate truth is indescribable and inexplicable; silence is an answer to questions about *dharma*. Yet, the same Zen masters often spoke out. They expounded *dharma* to their disciples and even urged them to study written conundrums, *kung-an*. How could they be silent and open at the same time? It seems that Zen Buddhists have done this by means of the twofold truth. From a transcendental perspective, one should keep silent even about the most important issues of suffering, its origin, cessation and the way leading to its cessation. In the *Twelve Gate Treatise*, when someone asked the Buddha, "Is suffering made by itself?"

the Buddha kept silent and did not answer. "World-honored! If suffering is not made by itself, is it made by another?" The Buddha still did not answer. "World-honored! Is it made by itself and by another?" The Buddha remained silent. "World-honored! Is it then made by no cause?" The Buddha still did not answer. Thus, as the Buddha did not answer these questions, one should know that all things are empty.[32] Mādhyamika recognition of the Buddha's silence may have encouraged Zen Buddhists to emphasize "a special transmission outside the scriptures; no dependence upon words and letters."[33] This teaching also gave them the wisdom (*prajñā*) to keep silent. On the other hand, the Mādhyamika teaching of emptiness as the twofold truth would urge Zen Buddhists to use words and concepts to explain Buddha's *dharma* so that all sentient beings can be awakened. This enables them to display compassion and to live in transcendental and conditional worlds simultaneously. Due, then, to wisdom and compassion, Zen masters may have seemingly inconsistent or paradoxical teachings and practices.

IV. Zen and the Refutation of Erroneous Views as the Illumination of Right Views

The Mādhyamikas claimed that they did not hold any view and what they were doing was just to examine the opponents' theories and expose their fallacies. The so-called "right" and "wrong," or "true" and "false," in reality, are equally empty. For the Mādhyamikas, the refutation of erroneous views and the illumination of right views are not two different things but the same; to negate erroneous views does not require a new view, but merely the rejection of views. Hui-neng and other Zen Buddhists followed this model of teaching and held that *right* is "that which is without any view" and *wrong* is "that which is with some view."[34] Like the Mādhyamikas, Zen Buddhists claimed that there are no right, wrong, good or bad. One should think of neither good nor evil, and try neither to do good nor to avoid evil. A true Buddhist knows the emptiness of valuations and goes beyond true and false, right and wrong.[35]

Hui-neng and his followers seem to use the Mādhyamika teaching of the refutation of erroneous views as the illumination of right views to discuss the relation between meditation and wisdom. According to them, meditation is a device to eliminate erroneous views, while wisdom, which is supposed to illuminate right views, is really a convenient term for this device. Meditation and wisdom are not two separate things but one. People therefore should not emphasize the importance of meditation at the expense of wisdom, nor stress wisdom at the expense of meditation. Hui-neng said, "Learned audience, to what are meditation and wisdom analogous? They are analogous to a lamp and its light. With the lamp, there is light. Without it, it would be dark. The lamp is the quintessence of the light and the light is the expression of the lamp. In name they are two things, but in substance they are the same. It is the same case with meditation and wisdom."[36]

The essence of meditation, according to Hui-neng, is not to sit cross-legged but to get rid of delusion and passion. He once remarked, "While living one sits up and lies not; when dead, one lies and sits not; a set of ill-smelling skeleton! What is the use of toiling and moiling so?"[37] Once the mind is purified, meditation and wisdom would no longer be needed, so Zen may repudiate even *zen* (*ch'an*, meditation).

There are many parallel teachings in Zen and Mādhyamika, sufficient to show a great Mādhyamika influence upon Zen. It seems that Zen Buddhists followed San-lun Mādhyamika philosophy and used San-lun doctrines as a major philosophical basis in the creation and development of their religion. One who sees this will find that Zen Buddhism is really not so anti-philosophical and incomprehensible as it appears.

Chapter Four

The Mādhyamika Treatment
of Philosophical Issues

Philosophers have often considered their main task the description and explanation of the essence (whatness) or existence (thatness) of reality. Philosophy is often defined as the study of the true nature of things. Idealism, materialism, pluralism, monism, nihilism, absolutism, theism and atheism are theories about what really is. Some emphasize the permanent and abiding aspect of experience and hold that the nature of things is unchanging. Others emphasize the impermanent, changing and momentary aspect of experience and contend that reality is pure flux. Generally speaking, in the Western tradition the former static view of the universe can be seen in Parmenides' philosophy and the dynamic view in Heraclitus. In the Indian tradition, the former, represented by Brāhmanism, is known as the *ātman* view, and the latter, represented by Hīnayāna Buddhism, is known as the *anātman* view.

Philosophy for the Mādhyamikas is not the description and explanation of the true nature of things. Nāgārjuna analyzed both the *ātman* and *anātman* views and declared that all metaphysical systems are dogmatic. The Mādhyamika argued that speculation does not give knowledge but illusion. True wisdom is the abandonment of views.

Mādhyamika philosophy exposes the implications of the major concepts of traditional philosophers. Nāgārjuna seemed to find that philosophers manufacture problems by asking unintelligible questions. One important point that he and Chinese followers such as Chi-tsang wanted to convey is that traditional philosophy is a disease. The cause of the disease is an erroneous view of the role of concepts and words, and the cure lies not in finding a new metaphysics, but in knowing the proper nature and function of conceptualization. According to the Mādhyamika, the Buddha's emptiness is a medicine for curing the disease of conceptual thinking. It teaches that concepts and words are empty, and warns that men are enslaved to language they create and use.[1] To achieve enlightenment, one should eliminate conceptualization.[2]

Unfortunately, people, according to the Mādhyamika, cannot see the emptiness of concepts and words. They often believe that concepts and words stand for certain extra-linguistic objects or entities, and that the meaning of a term is the object. For them, to see the meaning of a conceptual device or statement is to find an extra-linguistic entity, and to know truth is to search for reality. Knowledge is the knowing of things; epistemology is believed to be dependent upon metaphysical assumptions. If a true statement does not refer to an empirical phenomenon, it must denote or point to non-empirical or absolute reality. So philosophers are often led unsuspectingly into metaphysical disputes about such questions as: Is reality òne or many? Is it permanent or impermanent? Is there a God who created all realities? Such philosophers regard these metaphysical questions as genuine and develop various theories to resolve the disputes.

The Mādhyamika way of emptiness is an observation that traditional Indian philosophers had been misled by concepts and failed to see that such metaphysical questions are not genuine. Hence they wasted their time in establishing a metaphysical theory. By this light, orthodox Buddhist philosophers had the same disease as Hindu philosophers. They did not give up the conceptual way of thinking but merely changed position from the static view of the universe to the dynamic view. The Hīnayāna *anātman* philosophy, according to the Mādhyamika, appears to be better than *ātman* philosophy, but actually is as untenable as the Hindu standpoint. It cannot resolve the metaphysical dispute. The true solution is not to present a new view, but to stop conceptual thinking. This is what the Mādhyamikas mean when they say that they have no view.

In expounding this point, the Mādhyamikas state an important discovery: to look for the meaning of a term is not to look for an object, entity or essence, because meaning is a human projection. Right knowledge is not right understanding of some thing, but rather to understand that things are empty. Nor does the examination of epistemological issues necessarily presuppose or entail a metaphysical or ontological substance. If anyone fails to see this and considers emptiness as referring to an ontological or absolute entity, he cannot be "cured."[3]

Ātman, *dharmas* and other ontological entities, according to the Mādhyamikas, are nothing but objectified concepts. Their philosophy of emptiness denies projection of these concepts onto the world. Their dialectic is a critique of concepts rather than a metaphysical assertion.

I. The Problem of Reality

The problem of reality has been a main issue among Indian philosophers. Traditional Hindus and Buddhists have often made an ontological commitment to a thing or things and consider it the reality of the universe. The Mādhyamika philosophy of emptiness aims to show that these ontological realities cannot be established and are really objectified concepts. Any commitment to them is an attachment to be eliminated. By investigating the notion of *ātman*, *dharmas*, motion, rest and causality, the Mādhyamika attempted to clear away the problem of reality.

Ātman (*Self, I or Person*)

It is commonly believed that there is a permanent and abiding entity in man that persists through physical changes, exists before birth and after death, and remains from one life to another. It is called the soul, ego, self, I or person. In Indian tradition it is usually called *ātman*.[4] According to Brāhmanism, *ātman* "neither is born nor dies. It has not come from anywhere, has not become anyone. Unborn, constant, eternal, primeval, it is not slain when the body is slain."[5] *Ātman* is not only the feeler of sensations, thinker of thoughts, and receiver of rewards and punishments for actions good and bad, but is ontologically identical with *Brāhman*, the essential reality underlying the universe.

According to the Mādhyamikas, the Brahmanical *Ātman-Brāhman* philosophy is untenable. Their main criticism is not that it is false but unintelligible. They argue not only that there is no *ātman* but that there could not conceivably be any such entity.

Traditional Hindu philosophers seem to assume that what is real must be permanent, unchanging and independent. Empirical phenomena are often considered too transient to be real; reality is absolute *ātman*. For the Mādhyamika, this philosophy raises certain serious conceptual problems. It seems that there do appear changing phenomena in the universe, yet if being real means unchanging and self-subsistent, what sort of things are these phenomena? Are they merely illusions, or characteristics or attributes of *ātman*? If changing phenomena are illusions, there would be no real production, origination, decay and destruction, and hence the continuity of a life would be impossible. No evil person could be transformed. Moral disciplines would lose their significance and spiritual effort would be in vain. But this seems absurd. If changing phenomena are characteristics of *ātman*, what is the precise relationship between *ātman* and the characteristics? Is *ātman* identical with the characteristics or different? If identical, *ātman* would be subject to birth, death and destruction since the phenomena, our bodies or physical appearances, are subject to them. This would contradict the very notion of *ātman*.[6] If *ātman*, on the other hand, is different from the characteristics, it would be perceived without characteristics. But it is not so perceived because nothing can be perceived to exist without characteristics. Actually, a thing without any characteristic is, in principle, indefinable and hence inconceivable.[7]

It may be argued that the *ātman* exists behind, beneath or underlying changing characteristics, and that although the *ātman* differs from the characteristics and cannot be perceived directly, its existence can be inferred. For example, fire is different from smoke, yet we can know fire exists by perceiving smoke. However, for the Mādhyamika, inference and analogy are inapplicable in the case of knowing the *ātman*. In principle we cannot directly perceive the *ātman* while in principle we can directly perceive fire. When there is no smoke, we know there is a fire by seeing it, but we cannot see the *ātman* when there are no characteristics. Therefore, the example is not adequate. The Mādhyamikas accentuate that inference and analogy are applicable among directly perceivable phenomena, but not between indirectly perceivable noumena. So it is unintelligible to say that *ātman* exists behind changing appearances.[8]

Nāgārjuna argued that nothing has selfhood, that *ātman* is empty. However, his critique is stated from the standpoint of a higher truth. He did not deny that we have an idea of the self, when viewed from the conventional standpoint, as a collection of different states or characteristics, and that the self and characteristics are mutually dependent.[9] He did deny that the *ātman* is permanent, abiding, unchanging and self-existing.

This denial is essentially a critique of the thesis that what is real must be defined as permanent and independent.

Dharmas (Elements or Constituents of Experience)

For early scholastic Buddhists the Buddha's teaching of *anātman* (non-self) does not mean that all things are empty, but that the true state of things is momentary, particular and multiple. Like non-Buddhist philosophers, Hīnayāna philosophers engaged in the examination of the reality of the universe. They analyzed the world into basic components and regarded them as the fundamental constituents of the world. These are the truly real events in the universe and are called *dharmas*. For scholastic Buddhists, all complex phenomena in the world can be reduced to or composed of *dharmas*. Although each *dharma* is not supported by substance or self, and exists for an instant,[10] it has its own or independent nature (*svabhāva, tzu-hsing*). *Dharmas* are distinct and separate, yet appear and disappear in accordance with the principle of causality. They are classified into *skandhas, āyatanas* and *dhātus*. The *skandhas* are the five constituents of a person or self. *Āyatanas* are the six sense organs, including mind, and their respective spheres. *Dhātus* are variously six or eighteen, and include earth, air, water, fire, space and consciousness.[11]

The Mādhyamikas argue that it is fallacious to affirm the reality of momentary entities; the concept of *dharma* is as unintelligible as *ātman*. Nāgārjuna offered two main arguments to show that the *dharma* theory is untenable. He first argued that the claim "*dharmas* exist" is contradictory or absurd. He analyzed the meaning of the word *existence*; in close examination of experience we find that whatever can be conceived to exist has a cause. All things are produced by a combination of various causes and conditions. When the conditions change, things will also change and even disappear. *To exist* means to be caused, conditioned, generated or dependent on something. But by definition a *dharma* is an entity which has its own or independent nature.[12] So to say that a *dharma* exists would be the same as saying that an independent thing is dependent. This is a contradiction in terms.[13]

Nāgārjuna also argued that a momentary entity or impermanent *dharma* is a contradiction in terms. He pointed out that what is impermanent and momentary can be divided into non-enduring or non-abiding moments and has, analytically, no duration whatever.[14] It disappears as soon as it appears. Therefore it cannot be said to have true existence.[15] However, an entity, being or object is supposed to have some duration. So, to say that an entity is impermanent is tantamount to saying that what abides is non-abiding; this is contradictory.

It might be argued that we cannot understand impermanence as non-duration only. When we say that something is impermanent, we mean that it arises, endures for a moment and then ceases to be. The reality of the phenomenal is that all things have such characteristics as origination, duration and cessation.[16] Therefore it is not absurd to say that there exist impermanent *dharmas* which possess duration.

But, Nāgārjuna contended, if this is the reality of the phenomenal, how do characteristics characterize a *dharma*? Do they characterize it simultaneously or successively? If simultaneously, there would be contradiction or confusion[17] because origination, duration and cessation are opposed by nature: At the time of cessation there should not be duration, and at the time of duration there should not be cessation. Further, they cannot be said to characterize an object successively because if the characteristics occur at different times, there would be three different phenomena. How can different phenomena be true of the "same" thing?[18]

According to Nāgārjuna, the *dharma* theory raises many other conceptual problems. Are the three characteristics created (*samskrta*) or non-created (*asamskrta*)? If each characteristic is created, it too should have the three characteristics of origination, duration and cessation. These three characteristics, like other created things, should also each have three characteristics, and this would go on *ad infinitum*. On the other hand, if each characteristic is non-created, how can it characterize a created thing?[19]

Moreover, what is the relation between an object and characteristics? Is the object identical or different from the characteristics? If identical, there would be no distinction between them, and it would be absurd to say that the one is object and the other, characteristics. Perhaps one might say that characteristics have the object as their substance and are its manifestation, and in this sense the two are identical. According to Nāgārjuna, this is to say that the relation between characteristics and object is reflexive, yet there cannot be reflexive relations. If there were a reflexive relation, a thing would be subject and object at the same time. This is clearly impossible because subject and object are different. On the other hand, if a thing is different from characteristics, there would be no internal connection between them. How can we then say that characteristics characterize objects?[20]

Upholders of the *dharma* theory assume the reality of motion or change, whereas Nāgārjuna contended that motion itself cannot be established. If motion is impossible, it makes little sense to describe reality as impermanent, changing and multiple. Nāgārjuna's argument for the impossibility of motion is well stated in the *Middle Treatise* and was restated by the Chinese Mādhyamika Seng-chao in the *Chao-lun*. Actually, Nāgārjuna's entire *Twelve Gate Treatise* argues the impossibility of a similar theme, origination or production (*sheng*).

The Impossibility of Motion and Rest

Since the beginning of philosophical speculation in Western thought the concept of motion has played an important role. Heraclitus is famous for the statement, "All things are in a state of flux."[21] Heraclitus viewed motion as the cosmological principle underlying physical reality. By contrast, Zeno and other

Greek Eleatics denied the reality of motion. Zeno's famous antinomies of Achilles and the arrow aim to refute the possibility of motion.[22] The concept of motion has also been an important issue in Eastern philosophy. According to the realistic school of the Vaiśeṣikas, motion is one of three things in which the genus existence inheres, the other two being substance and quality.[23] Motion is different from the thing moving, as exemplified by the fact that the conjunction of the thing with its place has been destroyed and a new conjunction with a new place produced. Vaiśeṣikas accepted motion as duration, lasting until the cessation of motion. Early Buddhists, generally speaking, held that everything is in perpetual flow—reality is pure flux. They denied the existence of mental substance or mover behind the movement, but asserted that all created things are changing and have the characteristics of origination, duration and cessation. However, some early Buddhists, such as the Sammitīya and the Vātsīputrīya, accepted not only motion but a real mover or mental substance behind movement.

In Mādhyamika philosophy, motion and rest are empty: Their natures cannot be rationally explained. Like Zeno, Nāgārjuna examined the possibility of motion critically. He showed that the terms *moving*, *mover* and *path of moving* do not refer to realities which have specific characteristics or natures. And while Zeno affirmed the reality of rest, Nāgārjuna questioned its possibility also.

Nāgārjuna's critical analysis of the concepts of motion and rest is, in fact, a part of his campaign against all metaphysical views. For him, to say that something is moving is wrong, and to say that something is not moving is also wrong. Both the dynamic and static views of the universe should be refuted. This was an essential message in the Buddha's teaching of the middle way.

When Nāgārjuna discussed motion and rest, he dealt with four main issues or problems: (I) Motion cannot be established, (II) The mover or moving entity cannot be established,

(III) The path of motion cannot be established, (IV) Rest cannot be established. Nāgārjuna explicated each of them as follows:[24]

(I) Motion is not possible and cannot be established. Nāgārjuna pointed out that without motion the divisions of space as the traversed, the yet-to-be-traversed and so forth cannot be made. On the other hand, without these divisions motion itself cannot be understood. When we examine the path of motion, we see that it consists of (a) the part which is already passed (*i-ch'u*, *gata*) and (b) the part which is yet to be passed (*wei-ch'u*, *agata*). When we examine the part which is already passed, we do not find the act of passing in it because it has already been passed. Nor do we find the act of passing in the part which is yet to be passed because it is not yet. So the act of passing is impossible.

It may be argued that the existence of a path which has neither been passed nor is yet to be passed is not beyond comprehension because there is "the path which is being passed" (*ch'ü-shih*, *gamyamāna*), and here motion occurs. Nāgārjuna contended that one can say there is "the path which is being passed" if and only if there is the act of passing. But if we are still examining whether there is the act of passing, how can we use "the path which is being passed" to establish the act of passing?

It might also be argued that we see that things "begin" to move, hence we cannot deny the reality of motion. However, Nāgārjuna contended that the beginning of motion is not possible. He asked, "Where does motion begin, and when does it start? Does it begin at the place which is already passed, or at the place which is yet to be passed, or at the place which is being passed?" There cannot be a "beginning to pass" at "the place or moment which is already passed," because the latter is the effect of the former. But the latter is over, how can there be a former? Nor can there be a "beginning to pass" at "the place which is yet to be passed," for the former is the starting point of change. The latter has no change yet, and hence there cannot be a "beginning to pass" in it. The "place which is being passed" is possible only if there is the act of passing, and the act of passing is possible only if there is the beginning of passing, so we cannot use "the place which is being passed" to justify the reality of the beginning of passing. His argument can be summarized as follows:

(1) Motion must start at some place or at some time.
(2) But motion cannot start at that which is already passed.
(3) Neither can it start at that which is yet to be passed.
(4) Nor can it start at that which is being passed.
(5) There is no other place or time at which motion can start.
(6) Therefore, motion cannot start.

(II) The mover cannot move. It seems that this section is given mainly to criticize the Sammitīya and the Vātsīputrīya. According to these early Buddhists, motion is possible since there is a mover or moving entity. But Nāgārjuna asked, if someone moves, does "the one who has already moved" move or is it "the one who has not yet moved"? We cannot say that "the one who has not yet moved" moves because that involves contradiction. Neither can we say that "the one who has already moved" moves because his action is over.

Perhaps it may be said that the mover means "the one who is moving." Since there is the one who is moving, motion is possible. For Nāgārjuna, however, this consideration does not help. He pointed out that there can be a mover only when there is an act of moving, yet whether there is an act of moving is the issue we are examining. So we cannot use the mover to prove the existence of motion without begging the question. If one still insists that the mover moves, he would commit two fallacies: one, that the mover can be separated from the act of moving, and the other, that there are two kinds of motion, namely, motion in the mover and motion in the act of moving.

For Nāgārjuna, the question of whether the mover can move is concerned with the problem of substance-attribute relations. Suppose both the mover and motion are real. What is their relation? Is the mover identical or different from the motion? If identical, then actor and action are the same, and the mover would always be moving. Similarly, an eater would always be eating. This is absurd. If on the other hand the mover is different from motion, then the mover can exist without motion, and vice versa. This is also absurd. So Nāgārjuna held that neither motion nor the mover could be established.

(III) The path of motion cannot be established. As we have seen that motion and the mover cannot be established, Nāgārjuna argued that the path of motion is also impossible. Since motion cannot even be started, how can we talk about a place to go?

(IV) Rest cannot be established. One might argue that since there is no motion, no mover and no path of motion, there must be rest and thereby contend that, since rest is the cessation of motion, the reality of rest assumes the reality of motion. But for Nāgārjuna the denial of motion does not entail the affirmation of rest. Nāgārjuna's analysis runs as follows: Suppose rest is real. There must be someone or something that rests. Now who or what rests? Does the mover (the moving thing) or the non-mover (the non-moving thing) rest? It is absurd to say that the mover rests because this involves contradiction. Perhaps it may be said that the mover rests when he stops moving. But Nāgārjuna asked, "How can this be?" When someone stops moving, he is not the mover anymore, so we cannot say that the mover rests. On the other hand, we cannot say that the non-mover rests either, because rest means the cessation of motion. But the non-mover does not move, so how can he cease to move (rest)? Besides the mover and non-mover there is none other that rests. So rest is impossible. Nāgārjuna's argument can be briefly stated:

(1) If rest is real, there must be someone (or something) that rests.
(2) But the mover (or the moving thing) cannot rest.
(3) Neither can the non-mover (or the non-moving thing) rest.
(4) Besides the mover and the non-mover there is none other that can rest.
(5) Therefore rest is impossible.

Nāgārjuna gave another argument against the possibility of rest. If rest is real, it must happen at some place or at some time. Nāgārjuna asked, "Where or when can this happen?" Will it happen at that which is already passed (or the past), or at that which is yet to be passed (or the future), or at that which is being passed (or the present)? But as pointed out previously, there cannot be motion in any one of these situations, hence there cannot be the cessation of motion or rest.

Thus rest cannot be established, and one cannot use it to establish the existence of motion. For Nāgārjuna, motion and rest are relative to each other, hence both are devoid of specific character or nature, and neither is real. Therefore, one cannot hold that what is real is permanent or impermanent, and consequently one cannot maintain either the dynamic or static interpretations of the universe.

The Emptiness of Causality

The central message of the Buddha—suffering, its origin, its cessation and the way leading to its cessation—is directly concerned with causality. The Buddha is reported to have said, "He who sees the *pratītyasamutpāda* (causality or dependent co-arising) sees the *Dharma*, and he who sees the *Dharma*, sees the *pratītyasamutpāda*."[25] Accepting the Buddha's statement,[26] Mādhyamikas used *pratītyasamutpāda* to refute erroneous views and identified with emptiness and the middle way, but they did not accept causality as the governing principle of all phenomena or "the nature of reality."[27] The concept of causality as cosmic reality is, for the Mādhyamika, as untenable as the concepts of *ātman*, *dharmas*, motion and rest. Their doctrine of *Śūnyatā* is not only a doctrine of *ātman-śūnyatā* and *dharma-śūnyatā*, but also *pratītyasamutpāda-śūnyatā*. The first point Nāgārjuna made in the *Twelve Gate Treatise* was that causality is neither rationally justifiable nor empirically verifiable.

The principle of *pratītyasamutpāda* is given in the traditional formula:

When this is, that is;
This arising, that arises;
When this is not, that is not;
This ceasing, that ceases.[28]

Frequently *this* and *that* in the formula are interpreted as referring to this entity and that entity which possess self-nature. Early scholastic Buddhists seemed to follow this ontological interpretation of the causal relation governing constituents of the universe. For them, whatever exists is a cause; cause and existence are synonymous.

Hīnayāna Buddhists used the notion of causation to describe both moral and physical phenomena. The principle shows necessary connections between events and can be stated as moral law and physical law. When enunciated as a moral law, it means that there are good deeds and their rewards, and bad deeds and punishment. When stated as a physical law, it means that every fact is conditioned by or dependent on something else. *Pratītyasamutpāda* is the causal law regulating the rise and fall of all *dharmas*.[29] Classically, there are four external causal conditions and twelve internal causal conditions[30] enumerated in early Buddhist treatises. Each of these is conditioned (*paṭiccasamppanna*) as well as conditioning (*paṭiccasamuppāda*).[31] When viewed from the antecedent cause, each is an effect, but when viewed from its effect, it is a cause. The entire sequence should be considered as a circle, not as a chain. The cycle of twelve causal conditions pictures the wheel of existence.

Early Buddhists believed the principle of causality to be objectively, necessarily, eternally and universally valid.[32] According to Nāgārjuna, *pratītyasamutpāda* as the objective law governing all things can be stated only from the standpoint of conventional truth. Ordinary experience seems to show that things or events are never found alone, but always together with others which constitute their circumstances and causal conditions. However, were we to try to discover what a causal relation or process actually is, the intellect would be baffled.

Nāgārjuna argued that it is impossible to explain the relationship between cause and effect because any view of causation leads to contradictions or absurdity. In his writings he considered the following possibilities:[33]

(1) An effect is real in a cause (or an assemblage of causes and conditions), or an effect is unreal in a cause.

(2) A cause gives to an effect a causal nature before it ceases to be, or a cause does not give to an effect a causal nature before it ceases.

(3) A cause and an effect appear together simultaneously, or a cause and an effect do not appear together simultaneously.

(4) A cause becomes an effect, or a cause does not become an effect.

(5) A cause is within an effect, or an effect is within a cause.

(6) A cause is identical to an effect, or a cause is different from an effect.[34]

Generally speaking, Nāgārjuna criticized each relation more or less the same way. Here, the first relationship will be discussed briefly to show how he analyzed *pratītyasamutpāda*.

Nāgārjuna used the tetralemma to posit: (a) An effect is already real in a cause, (b) an effect is unreal in a cause, (c) an effect is both real and unreal in a cause. He argued that none of these could be established, and thus theories of causality should be renounced.

If there is a causal relation among things in the universe, Nāgārjuna asked, what is that relation? We cannot say that an effect is already real in a cause and is produced by the cause because if an effect were already real in a cause, why must it be produced again? That which has been done does not need to be done, and that which has been achieved does not need to be achieved. Nothing new is produced and hence there cannot be a causal production. If there were causal production, there might be sons, grandsons, great-grandsons and great-great-grandsons in the womb of a mother because effects are, in principle, already real in a cause. This is clearly absurd. If an effect were already real in a cause, the so-called cause would be only a location and should not be called a cause.

On the other hand, if an effect is at the outset unreal in a cause and yet is produced by the cause, then in principle anything should be capable of being produced from anything else. For example, carts, horses, food and other things could be produced from string. If something can be produced from nothing, why are rugs and not carts produced from string? Actually, if an effect is at the outset unreal in a cause, there would be no particular or distinct relation between the two, and hence one would not be the cause of the other.[35]

The third view, that an effect is both real and unreal in a cause, is also untenable. "For real and unreal are contradictory in nature. How can things that are contradictory in nature be together?"[36]

Finally, to say that an effect is neither real nor unreal in a cause is tantamount to accepting that there is no causal relation between cause and effect. If there is no causal relation, how can one be called a cause and the other an effect? So one cannot say that an effect is neither real nor unreal in a cause.[37]

Thus Nāgārjuna refuted causal theory to show that causality is empty. It might be argued that, although a causal relation cannot be established on logical or rational grounds, it can be established by experience. For example, he wrote, when we examine past experience we see that sesame oil is always produced from sesame, never from sand. Experience justifies our claim that there is no causal relation between sesame oil and sand. Hence we seek sesame oil in sesame, not in sand. For Nāgārjuna, however, the principle of causation cannot be justified even by experience. An observation of the constant conjunction of events does not justify a principle of causation, rather it begs the question.

If causation had been established, then we could say that, since we have seen sesame produce sesame oil but have never seen sand produce sesame oil, we seek sesame oil in sesame but not in sand. However, causation or production has not yet been established, and so one cannot legitimately make that claim. To employ the example that we have seen sesame produce oil is based upon the very notion of causation which is to be established. In short, according to Nāgārjuna, any empirical justification of causation assumes the principle it tries to prove.

Nāgārjuna also questioned ontological interpretation of causation. He argued that it is unintelligible to hold that there are entities in causal conditions.[38] He asked, "How is it possible for an entity which has essential nature to be something which is caused?"[39] This involves contradiction because *to be caused* is to be conditioned or to be dependent. However, an entity is supposed to have essential nature and a thing of essential nature is not produced but independent of other things.[40] If an entity is caused, it is dependent. Again this is impossible, and accordingly the causal principle cannot be the causal principle of entities.

As has been pointed out, early Buddhists considered the principle of causation a moral as well as physical law. For a good deed there must be a reward, and for a bad one, a punishment. The Mādhyamika argued that necessary connections between good deeds and rewards, and bad deeds and punishment, cannot be rationally explained.[41] They are not objective laws in nature or society, but subjective projections of the mind. Nāgārjuna wrote, "Defilements, *karmas*, doers, rewards, and punishments are all similar to a mirage, a dream, a shadow of light and an echo of voice."[42]

According to the Mādhyamika, the principle of *pratītyasamutpāda* should be understood as a soteriological device presented by the Buddha to help men achieve enlightenment or *nirvāṇa*. It lets people know that all things are empty because all things are causes and effects, and hence devoid of self-nature.[43] Thereby, it helps dispel notions of *ātman*, *dharma*s and other things. It also serves to keep one from falling into eternalism or nihilismm. *Pratītyasamutpāda* performs the same soteriological function as emptiness and the middle way; hence Nāgārjuna once said:

It is *pratītyasamutpāda* that we call emptiness; it is a provisionary name; it is also the middle way.[44]

Here we must acknowledge, however, that Nāgārjuna did not deny that, from the practical, conventional point of view, all things are produced from causes and conditions. What he did deny is that the causal principle can be justified and that it is the ultimate principle of the universe.

II. The Problem of God

Nāgārjuna is often said to have given a special status to the *Tathāgata* and exposed pantheism or some form of theism. In his famous *The Central Philosophy of Buddhism*, T.R.V. Murti wrote:

> [The Mādhyamika hold that] all beings have also to be considered as God; Buddha [Gautama] is not the only instance of man attaining perfection. Absolutism translated in terms of religion can only be a Pantheism. It is necessarily committed to the unity of all beings, the identity of God and man and the transcendence of the Absolute.[45]

Recently, he made the following statement:

> Nowhere does the Mādhyamika concern itself directly with issues like god, soul, matter, creation, etc.[46]

In fact, Nāgārjuna *does* discuss such problems as God, creation and making in the *Twelve Gate Treatise*, a work that unfortunately exists only in Chinese. The following presentation summarizes his treatment and will suggest a Mādhyamika view of God which is neither theism, atheism, agnosticism or pantheism.

A Critique of God as Creator
The word *God* has been used in a great many senses. In Buddhism the main admirable characteristics of God or divine being are omnipotence, omniscience, omnipresence, perfect goodness and always loving. When the Buddha was deified as God, these characteristics were ascribed to him.[47] Generally speaking, the Buddha has not been considered the creator of the universe. However, certain non-Buddhists, according to

Nāgārjuna, believe in the existence of God as the creator, ruler, and destroyer of the world and call Him Ĩsvara.[48] For these people, the question of how *kalpa* or the world were made is genuine, and God is used in answer. One may wonder whether it is entirely warranted for Nāgārjuna to identify the traditional Indian philosophers' concept of Ĩsvara with God. However, we should bear in mind that Nāgārjuna was less concerned with a description of the Indian Ĩsvara than with a critical analysis of the concept of a deity.

The Mādhyamika do not assert that the existence of God is false or doubtful, but that God's existence as the creator of the world is unintelligible. Nāgārjuna presented several arguments to show that creation, making, production or origination are ultimately empty, and that *creator*, *maker*, *producer* and *originator* are not genuine names referring to reality. Accordingly, it is unintelligible to assert the existence of God as the creator or maker of the universe.

Nāgārjuna examined the meaning and the possibility of "Something is made or produced by someone or something." He pointed out that whenever we say, "Something is made or produced by someone or something," either (1) x is made by itself, (2) x is made by another, (3) x is made by both, or (4) x is made from no cause at all. Yet none of these cases can be established, therefore the proposition cannot be established, and hence it makes no sense to say that the world was made by God.

He first argued that x cannot be made by itself. If it makes itself, it makes its own substance. However, a thing cannot use itself to make itself because there cannot be a genuine reflexive action. Were there reflexive action, a thing would be both subject and object at once, and this is impossible because subject and object are different.

Conventionally we think that things are made or produced by causal conditions. In this context the conditions or causes would be called "other," thus a thing is made by another.

Nāgārjuna countered that if an object is produced from conditions, it has the conditions as its substance. The object and conditions would have the same substance and would be the same. Accordingly, the conditions should not be called "other." Thus x cannot be conceived to be made by another.

Nor can a thing be said to be made by both itself and another. If made by both, this implies that both the object and the other have the power of producing the object. But as previously pointed out, neither has the power of producing. So x cannot be conceived to be made by both. Nor can a thing be said to be made by no cause. If a thing is produced from no cause at all, there would be a fallacy of eternalism.[49] Nāgārjuna concluded that the statement "Something is made or produced by someone or something" cannot be established. By this, he showed why the question of the making or creation of something is not a genuine question and also why the assertion of the existence of God as the maker or creator of all things is not intelligible.

In the last chapter of the *Twelve Gate Treatise*, Nāgārjuna examined the issue from another angle. If there is the fact of producing, making or creating, what produces (or what is produced)?: (a) Does "that-which-is-already-produced" (*sheng*) produce? (b) Does "that-which-is-not-yet-produced" (*wei-sheng*) produce? (c) Does "that-which-is-being-produced" (*sheng-shr*) produce? Nāgārjuna argued that (a), (b) and (c) could be refuted in the same way as the concept of motion.[50] Since production, origination, making or creation as such cannot be established, it makes no sense to say that there is Īśvara or God who produced, originated or created the universe.

The Mādhyamika criticism of theological conclusions resembles certain contemporary criticism concerning the existence of God. Contemporary philosophers have attended to the meaningfulness of theological statements and condemned as senseless such questions as: What is the explanation of the origin of the universe? Who is the creator of all things? How was the world made? In a debate with F.C. Copleston about the existence of God,[51] Bertrand Russell argued that the question "What is the explanation of the origin of the universe?" is as senseless as the question "Who is the mother of the human race?" It makes sense, he said, to inquire after the origin of a particular phenomenon, but not to ask for an explanation of the origin of the entire universe. Russell told Father Copleston, "I can illustrate what seems to be your fallacy. Every man who exists has a mother, and it seems to me your argument is that therefore the human race must have a mother, but obviously the human race hasn't a mother—that's a different logical sphere."[52] According to Russell, it is illegitimate to ask the question of the cause of the world and hence it is nonsensical to question the existence of God.

The Mādhyamikas would agree with these negative criticisms, but their standpoint seems even more critical than Russell's. For Russell, the concept of cause or origin is applicable to the particular or individual, although not to the whole. It makes sense to demand an explanation of the origins of particular phenomena. The question of the production or making of something is still a genuine question. However, the Mādhyamikas extend the inapplicability of the concept of cause or origin to the particular as well. As has been shown, the so-called production of even particular phenomena is incomprehensible.

Further Arguments against the Existence of God

Nāgārjuna presented several other arguments in the *Twelve Gate Treatise* to refute the existence of God.[53] If God made all creatures, where did he create them? Was the place where he performed creation created by him? Was it created by another? If it was created by God, then where did he create it? If he stayed in another place to create this place, who created the other place? There would be an infinite regress. If that place were created by another, there would be two Gods or creators. This could not be the case, therefore things in the universe are not created by God.

Furthermore, if God created all things, who created him? Not God himself because nothing can create itself. If he was created by another, he would not be self-existent. Moreover, if God had a cause and came from another, then this other would come from still other. There would be an infinite regress.

Theists tend to attribute characteristics of omnipotence, omniscience, perfection and self-sufficiency to the deity. In examining these aspects, Nāgārjuna discussed what philosophers call the problem of evil. He argued that the existence of evil in the world proves that God is either not omnipotent or not all good, therefore God does not exist. His reasoning: obviously, there is evil in the world, both moral evil and physical suffering. We find not only the fact of moral evil, but also the fact that evil men enjoy happiness and that good men suffer. It seems that God cannot prevent this, or else he can prevent it, but will not. If God cannot prevent evil he is not omnipotent, and if he can but will not, he is not all good. Now if God is not omnipotent, or not all good, then by definition he is not God. Therefore God cannot be conceived to exist.

If God is the sole omnipotent and omniscient creator of the world, there should have been no obstacle to the process of his creation and the world ought to have been created in its totality at one and the same time. However, the scripture of the Tīrthikas speak thus: God wanted to create all creatures, he practiced ascetic deeds and then created all creeping insects; again he practiced ascetic deeds and created winged birds; he practiced ascetic deeds and created men and heaven. If it were due to the practice of ascetic deeds that all these were produced, we should know that all things were produced from *karma* or causal conditions, not by God.

Finally, when someone asked Buddha the question whether the world was made by God, he did not answer.

Neither Theism nor Atheism

The true Mādhyamika approach to the problem of the existence of God appears neither theistic nor atheistic. It is not theistic because the Mādhyamikas do not assert "God exists," and it is not atheistic because they do not assert "God does not exist." They merely state that he cannot be *conceived* of as existing. Christianity begins with the assumption of God's existence and that religious knowledge is knowledge of Him. The Mādhyamikas do not assume God's existence and do not believe the assumption of an absolute is necessary for wisdom.

On the other hand, Nāgārjuna's denial of theism does not entail atheism. For Nāgārjuna, if theism is unintelligible, then so is atheism. If the assertion that there is a God is nonsensical, then the atheist's assertion that there is no God is equally nonsensical *since only a significant statement can be significantly negated or contradicted.* If some person A makes up a piece of nonsense, "There are five roundsquares on the table," then another person B who counters with the denial, "There are no roundsquares on the table," is just as guilty of nonsense. For the Mādhyamikas, atheism as well as theism, from the higher point of view, leads to absurdity.

This approach is also very different from the atheistic position of the Cārvāka and early Sāmkhya. According to the latter, questions about the origin of things in the world are genuine. They use material elements instead of God to answer these questions, and hence assert that God does not exist. For the Mādhyamikas, the original questions are not genuine. Whether God or material elements have to be used to answer the questions is not at issue. The atheist asserts non-existence; Nāgārjuna merely found the concept of God unintelligible.

In ruling out atheism as well as theism, the Mādhyamika position may seem to be agnostic. In a sense, this is true because both the Mādhyamika and the agnostic refrain from assertion. However, in the agnostic view we *do not know* whether or not God exists. It is an attitude of doubt and despair. For the Mādhyamikas, we *do know* that the question of whether or not God exists is unintelligible. It is an attitude of conviction. This conviction is a religious remedy for the unenlightened. Further, it is characterisic of agnostics to hold that the existence of God is possible; there is no good reason either to believe or disbelieve. The agnostic does not deny that the question whether or not God exists is a genuine question. According to the Mādhyamikas, all statements about the existence of God involve absurdity, and they might go further and declare agnosticism untenable because if a statement about the existence of God is unintelligible, then it is unintelligible to doubt as well as to deny.

At first sight the Mādhyamika treatment of the problem of God seems similar to the view of logical positivists, since both hold that the question is not genuine and that utterances on the subjects are nonsensical. However, the objectives and reasons for their conclusions differ. Logical positivists hope to convince us that the empirical is the only reality or the objective data we can accept. They make an "ontological" commitment to sense experience and use empirical phenomena as the standard by which they judge the real and unreal, or the true and false. They offer this principle of verification: a statement is meaningful if some sense experience would be relevant to the determination of its truth or falsehood. It is then maintained that *God* does not denote any empirical entity and is a pseudo-term. All statements about the existence and nature of God are not empirically verifiable and hence are meaningless.[54] By contrast, Mādhyamika philosophy hopes to free us from making any ontological commitments to anything whatsoever, even to empirical phenomena. For the Mādhyamikas, sense experience is as empty as transcendental reality. God is a pseudo-term not because it denotes no empirical object, but rather because the concept itself leads to absurdity or contradiction. From their standpoint, logical positivism would be a new dogmatic metaphysics, thus it should be ruled out.

Mādhyamika philosophy may also appear similar to the pantheistic philosophy of the Upaniṣads: both refuse to make a commitment to sense experience, and both negate any positive description of the ultimate state of things. But as we have seen, Mādhyamika negation is quite different from the "*neti, neti*" (not this, not that) expression of the Upaniṣads. The first is pure negation, while the second is negation for affirmation.

The Mādhyamika and Upaniṣads also have different theories of knowledge. For the Upaniṣads, an assumption of the absolute essence, *Ātman-Brāhman*, is necessary for wisdom. For the Mādhyamika, wisdom is not right understanding of an absolute reality or some thing, but rather to know that all things are empty. Those who would see the doctrine of emptiness as absolutism, and give a special status to the *Tathāgata*, would be subject to the same criticisms as advocates of the *ātman* view.[55]

Actually, to give the *Tathāgata* special privilege as transcendent or self-existing reality runs counter to the basic doctrines of *pratītyasamutpāda* (dependent co-arising) and *anitya* (impermanence). For the Mādhyamika, a pantheistic or any theological approach to the Buddha rather damages our understanding of the Buddha.[56] So it is inappropriate to say that Mādhyamika Buddhism is pantheism.

III. The Problem of Knowledge

In his major works Nāgārjuna did not offer what modern Western philosophers would call a theory of knowledge. However, his critique of metaphysical views contains interesting comments on epistemological issues. In arguing for the impossibility of conceptual descriptions of reality, he analyzed the nature of language, claiming that our words are empty and that language cannot be used to describe the true nature of things. More generally, the Mādhyamikas have examined these epistemological issues: (a) They discuss truth and present the doctrine of the twofold truth. For them, truth is not purely objective and no truth is absolutely true. Every true claim which is so, is so for a particular observer or is made from a particular standpoint. Its truth-value lies in whether it is an effective means to *nirvāṇa*. (b) The Mādhyamikas investigate the nature of negation and present the doctrine of the refutation of erroneous views as the illumination of right views. They argue that negation is not necessarily the negation of something real. (c) They examine the concept of *pramāṇas*, the means of true cognition or right knowledge. Nāgārjuna contended that objects of knowledge cannot be known, and that there is no way for us to be sure that our concepts accurately describe reality. (d) They study the relation between words and reality to show that words are empty of reality. (e) The Mādhyamikas analyze sentences into the subject-predicate form and examine the relation between subject and predicate. Nāgārjuna attempted to show that a predicate cannot truly be predicated of a subject, and thereby to demonstrate that language cannot be used to describe reality.

Quest for Truth

The question "What is truth?" has been important in Eastern and Western thought, and was the first topic the Buddha expounded in his first sermon on the Four Noble Truths. In Buddhist tradition, the Buddha's teachings are called *Dharma* (Truth). Buddhists have sought enlightenment by understanding the *Dharma* and have presented the *Dharma* in terms of the twofold truth (*erh-ti-kuan*) and the threefold truth (*san-ti-kuan*). The Buddhist teaching of the threefold truth was well developed by the Yogācāra, while the twofold truth was well expounded by Nāgārjuna and his Chinese San-lun followers.

Many contemporary Buddhist scholars hold that the epistemology of any Buddhist school must be based on its metaphysical assumptions. Nāgārjuna is said to have a special insight into reality, and his dialectic to have a "visionary aspect," namely, pointing to transcendental reality. In discussing the Mādhyamika analysis of the Four Noble Truths, Alex Wayman wrote:

> The four Holy Truths (*catvāri āryasatyanai*) have to be understood as included in these two: Nirodhasatya as Nirvāṇa is paramārtha; and the other three, including the marga, are within samvṛti.... A most important feature of this distribution of the Four Noble Truths to the two truths is the fact that the Truth of Cessation is described from early Buddhism onwards as "realized directly" (sākṣāt, "before the eyes"), and so *paramārtha* by implication is realized by vision.[57]

Kenneth K. Inada has written:

> Thus the middle path is the "vision of the real in its true form...." Nāgārjuna...was the supreme Buddhist ontologist.[58]

Yet from my perspective on Chinese San-lun, the sources do not warrant an emphasis on Nāgārjuna's special insight into transcendental reality or his role as supreme ontologist. For Nāgārjuna and his San-lun disciples, the Buddha's *Dharma* is instrumental or functional in character; truths given by the Buddha do not aim to produce a vision of reality but to empty us of ontological attachment to anything, including *Dharma*.

The Pragmatic Nature of Truth

For Nāgārjuna and Chinese San-lun Buddhists, no reality is really real and no truth is truely true. In explicating these, Nāgārjuna engaged in epistemological dispute and used logical reasonings to refute all views. For him and San-lun Buddhists, truth and logic have no intrinsic value by themselves. They have place in the Buddha's *Dharma* simply because they are employed to eliminate attachment; without practical benefits, truth and logic would lose their meaning. According to the San-lun master Chi-tsang, they are merely provisionary instruments used to eradicate extreme views. People are often attached to some view and stick to some law. In order to free men from emotional and intellectual attachments, the Buddha preached certain "truth" and followed certain "logic." For the sake of repudiating the absolutist, the Buddha taught that existence is unreal, and to refute the nihilist he stated that existence is real.[59] Although *existence*, *real* and *unreal* are all empty, the Buddha's teachings can be regarded as truths so long as they can help dispel ignorance and illusion.[60] But when attachments and ignorance are removed, the truths are useless and so are not truths any more.[61] Thus all truths given by the Buddha, according to San-lun Buddhists, are pragmatic in nature and ultimately have to be dispensed with.[62]

The Mādhyamika treatment of truth appears similar to American pragmatism in that both schools of thought agree that truth cannot merely be a copy or right understanding of reality as such, but should have practical consequences. According to the Mādhyamika and the pragmatists, truth is not absolute, fixed, eternal. Metaphysical visions of reality, truth and falsity, apart from practical bearings are absurd. They both condemn what William James called "all noble, clean-cut, fixed, eternal, rational, temple-like systems of philosophy."[63] According to them our knowledge of the world is never absolutely true. Philosophy should be a way of critical inquiry, not a system of perfect truths. Mādhyamika Buddhism and pragmatism pay more attention to the method of philosophical investigation than to content. When they discuss the method and the principles of reasoning, they both reject the thesis that logical truths are *a priori* and eternally certain. Neither Mādhyamika nor the pragmatist thinks that logic provides us with truths independent of the human predicament. Rather, the validity of logic, in the strict sense of the word, lies in whether it can effectively solve life's problems.

Despite these apparent similarities, their philosophies are quite different. When William James claimed that truth must have practical consequences, he held that a basic or an important element of truth is satisfaction. "Satisfactoriness is what distinguished the true from the false," he wrote.[64] Truth is gained "by ever substituting more satisfactory for less satisfactory opinions."[65] He seemed to hold that passion provides a ground for a truth-claim: "Our passional nature not only lawfully may, but must, decide our option between propositions, whenever it is a genuine option that cannot by its nature be decided on intellectual grounds."[66]

According to the Mādhyamika, the Buddha's *Dharma* was given in part to remove desire. In Nāgārjuna's philosophy, the basic element of truth, especially of *paramārthasatya*, is not and should not be the satisfaction of our desires, interests and passions—instead, their elimination. Chi-tsang did not advance from one level to another to reach truth "by ever substituting more satisfactory for less satisfactory opinions." The progress he mentioned is rather the process of removing anything passional from the mind. The truth-value of the Buddha's teachings lies in their effectiveness as a means to the cessation of sense satisfaction, and ultimate truth is so called because it is devoid of any tinge of passion.

William James was committed to certain ontological realities or entities. In discussing the cognitive function of feeling and satisfactoriness, he wrote:

Well now, can our little feeling, thus left alone in the universe ...can the feeling, I say, be said to have any sort of a cognitive function? For it to *know*, there must be something to be known. What is there, on the present supposition?... Let us keep closer to the path of common usage, and reserve the name knowledge for the cognition of "realities," meaning by realities things that exist independently of the feeling through which their cognition occurs.[67]

The pragmatist calls satisfaction indispensable for truth-building, but I have everywhere called them insufficient unless reality is also incidentally led to.... For him, as for his critic, there can be no truth if there is nothing to be true about.[68]

James assumed the existence of realities,[69] which constitute the objective element of truth. Reality, for him, exists independently of our ideas and is known through a series of intermediary experiences. Knowledge or knowing is an "ambulatory" process[70] which involves the knowing mind, the object or reality known, and a series of intermediary experiences such as actions and thoughts which lead the mind to the object. To know something is to complete this process. An idea becomes true or comes to be true when it leads the mind through a series of experiences to the object. For James,

> "Truth,"...is a property of certain of our ideas. It means their agreement, as falsity means their disagreement, with reality.

> The truth of an idea is not a stagnant property inherent in it. Truth *happens* to an idea. It *becomes* true, is *made* true by events. Its verity *is* in fact an event, a process, the process namely of its verifying itself, its *verification*. Its validity is the process of its *validation*.[71]

Objectively, the ontological or material source of knowledge, for James, is what he called pure experience. He spoke of pure experience as "one primal stuff or material in the world, a stuff of which everything is composed,"[72] and wrote:

> "Pure experience" is the name which I gave to the immediate flux of life which furnishes the material to our later reflection with its conceptual categories. Only new-born babies, or men in semi-coma from sleep, drugs, illnesses, or blows, may be assumed to have an experience pure in the literal

sense of a *that*, which is not yet any definite *what*, tho' ready to be all sorts of whats.[73]

Thus, according to James, pure experience is the basic stuff of the world, natural until men cognize it.

From the Mādhyamika standpoint, James's analysis of the objective element of truth is not tenable. His commitment to reality is an attachment, and his concept of pure experience involves contradictions or absurdities. According to James's pragmatism, the only intelligible way of knowing the existence of something or of naming something is to complete what he called the ambulatory process. But his pure experience is prior to our ambulatory inspection. So to assume or to name pure experience is the same as having the ambulatory process in what is so far untouched by the ambulatory process. This is contradictory.

For James, pure experience is not a thing-in-itself, nor is it purely an idea. He described the basic stuff as "empirical reality" and called his philosophy epistemological realism: "This meant merely to exclude reality of an 'unknowable' sort, of which no account in either perceptual or conceptual terms can be given. It includes of course any amount of empirical reality independent of the knower. Pragmatism is thus 'epistemologically' realistic in its account."[74]

But when judged from the Mādhyamika Buddhist standpoint, the concept "empirical reality" is also unintelligible. What is empirical is supposed to be causally conditioned and is in a state of change. Hence it is devoid of its own nature, character or function or, for that matter, any definite nature, character or function. Yet reality is supposed to be something independent, having its own nature, character and function. Therefore, empirical reality means that what is devoid of its own nature is not so devoid, again contradictory.

According to the Mādhyamika, realities such as pure experience or empirical reality would be empty. Since reality cannot be established, it would make no sense to hold that an idea is true if it works satisfactorily in the sense that it successfully agrees with or corresponds serially with reality.

James's pragmatism is based on realism, but Nāgārjuna's epistemology does not presuppose any such metaphysical view. When the Mādhyamikas claim that an idea is true if it is useful, they merely mean that the idea can be accepted as true if it can effectively eradicate ignorance, illusion and attachment. When the Buddha made the statements "existence is real" and "existence is unreal" to refute nihilism and absolutism, his statements could be accepted as "truths" not because there are such ontological realities as "existence," "being" or "non-being" and the Buddha's ideas successfully agree with or lead to these realities or objects, but because the statements could effectively dispel metaphysical speculation.

In discussing the relationship between *true* and *useful*, James wrote, "You can say of it then either that 'it is useful because it is true' or that 'it is true because it is useful.' Both these phrases mean exactly the same thing, namely that here is an idea that gets fulfilled and can be verified."[75] According to San-lun Buddhists, *useful* may be a necessary but not a sufficient condition for an assertion to be true. There are many useful falsehoods and even useful absurdities. For example, the acceptance of naive realism is useful and beneficial in ordinary life. But naive realism is not only false but also unintelligible. Hence its denial is regarded as ultimate truth in Chi-tsang's philosophy.

Pragmatism is in part a technique for solving problems in philosophical or scientific inquiry, and has been particularly interested in finding the legitimate and clear meaning of concepts, ideas and words. The legitimate meaning of a concept becomes its practical, pragmatic bearing or consequence. Pragmatism is a method of determining the meaning of language, and its aim is to facilitate conceptual communication and find meaningful beliefs. According to James, pragmatism is really a method of clarifying and justifing truths. He wrote:

> Pragmatism...asks its usual question.... How will the truth
> be realized?... The moment pragmatism asks this question, it
> sees the answer: *True ideas are those that we can assimilate,
> validate, corroborate and verify. False ideas are those that
> we can not.*

> The verification of the assumption here means its leading to
> no frustration or contradiction.[76]

In a sense Nāgārjuna's philosophy is also a method rather than doctrine. But Nāgārjuna's dialectic is not a method of determining and clarifying the meaning of our conceptual schemes, but a method of devoiding of conceptualization. For Nāgārjuna words and names are empty.[77] Strictly speaking, no legitimate meaning of concepts, ideas and words can be found; all views involve contradictions or absurdities. And no means of cognition (*pramāṇa, liang*) can be established.[78] A true view is not any verified or justified view, but an absence of views. This teaching is stated by San-lun masters as *p'o-hsieh-hsien-cheng*: the refutation of wrong views is the illumination of right views. The aim of Nāgārjuna's dialectical method is to eliminate the conceptual way of thinking. A true Buddhist, according to the Mādhyamika, should not be committed or attached to anything, not even to the Four Noble Truths.

Prajñā as Non-knowing

Ultimately one should give up conceptualization and be silent. This silence is not the recognition of an absolute but the abandonment of attachments. For the Mādhyamika, the silence itself is essentially empty, and to realize this is *prajñā* (wisdom). *Prajñā* is not the knowing of anything substantial. In a strict sense it has no knowing or knowledge. Our ordinary mode assumes that there are acts of knowing, a knower and objects to be known; it also assumes a distinction between subject and object. To know is to search for something real in the world or the mind. For the Mādhyamika, this is really an intellectual attachment; the epistemological assertion implies an ontological commitment. *Prajñā* transcends this kind of knowing. It is an insight that the act of knowing, the knower, the object to be known and the distinction between subject and object are all empty.

Prajñā as non-knowing is a wisdom without attachment. It is really synonymous with *Śūnyatā*. This empty nature of *prajñā* was well stated by Seng-chao in the fifth century:

Real *prajñā* is as pure as empty space, without knowing, without seeing, without acting, and without objects. Thus knowledge is in itself without knowing, and does not depend on anything in order to be without knowledge....

So, when the *sūtra* says that *prajñā* is pure, it means that the essential nature of *prajñā* is really pure, fundamentally devoid of the knowing that apprehends deludedly. Since it is fundamentally devoid of the knowing that apprehends deludedly, it cannot be called "knowing." Not only lack of knowledge (no-knowing) is called no-knowledge (nonknowing), but knowledge (knowing) itself is no-knowledge (no-knowing)....

Thus in *prajñā* there is nothing that is known, and nothing that is seen.... It is evident that there is a markless knowing and unknowing illumination.[79]

The Buddha's *Dharma* has been given not to let men know anything, but to empty the mind so that they can achieve liberation from the evil and suffering of the world. This, according to the Mādhyamikas, is the purpose of the doctrine of emptiness.

Chapter Five

Nāgārjuna, Kant and Wittgenstein

Nāgārjuna's critique of metaphysical views has been likened to the philosophy of Immanuel Kant by some scholars. For example, T.R.V. Murti wrote:

> As the Mādhyamika goes straight to the issue in hand, the conflict in Reason, his objective too is very clear; namely, to condemn all conceptual patterns as relative (*śūnya*) and confine them to the empirical realm.... This corresponds to Kantian dictum about the transcendental ideality but empirical reality of the categories.[1]

The Mādhyamikas have examined the nature of language and argued for the emptiness of words. For Nāgārjuna, to look for the meaning of a word is not the same as looking for an object. Emptiness, according to San-lun masters, is empty in the sense that the word "emptiness" has no meaning by itself. Recently, many scholars have seemed to identify Nāgārjuna's philosophy with that of Ludwig Wittgenstein. For instance, Frederick J. Streng has asserted:

> Nāgārjuna's use of words for articulating Ultimate Truth would find champions in contemporary philosophers of the language analysis school such as Ludwig Wittgenstein....

The point of agreement between the second-century Buddhist philosopher and the contemporary language analyst is that metaphysical propositions do not provide the knowledge that is claimed by systematic metaphysicians. Words and expression-patterns are simply practical tools of human life, which *in themselves* do not carry intrinsic meaning and do not necessarily have meaning by referring to something outside the language system.[2]

It is said that Nāgārjuna never rejected the validity and legitimacy of the ordinary use of language, and his philosophy is designed to bring words back from their metaphysical to an everyday use. In Ives Waldo's words, "Nāgārjuna says nothing to counter the reply of the ordinary language philosopher that ordinary existence statements are paradigms of what we mean by 'true' and 'coherent'...."[3] In *Wittgenstein and Buddhism* Chris Gudmunsen even claimed, "All modern adherents of the Mādhyamika ought, in my submission, to be Wittgensteinians."[4]

I find Nāgārjuna philosophy quite different from Kant's and Wittgenstein's, and in fact, according to Chinese San-lun sources, Nāgārjuna did criticize the everyday use of language. Wittgenstein's understanding of language is not necessarily preferable to Nāgārjuna's, and in a sense Wittgensteinians ought to be Mādhyamikas, so that they can freely and creatively employ any means to examine philosophical and religious issues.

I. Nāgārjuna and Kant's Critique of Metaphysics

Kant became famous primarily because of his critique of metaphysics, but from Nāgārjuna's standpoint, Kant's philosophy would be considered metaphysical. Kant's idea of the noumenon is a metaphysical concept; he gave "the term noumena to things in themselves."[5] Although he denied the possibility of our knowledge of things in themselves, he acknowledged that we can think of them "under the title of an unknown something."[6] This unknown something was said to be "a merely limiting concept, the function of which is to curb the pretensions of sensibility."[7] However, it was regarded as something indispensable, for "The doctrine of sensibility is likewise the doctrine of the noumenon in the negative sense."[8] Our sensation, Kant contended, must have a cause, and the cause cannot be the subject, but must be the object, the thing-in-itself. Thus, although things-in-themselves are unknowable as they are in themselves, Kant held that "we know them through the representations which their influences on our sensibility procure for us."[9]

From Nāgārjuna's vantage, the concept of the thing-in-itself as an unknown something would be subject to the same criticism as the Hindu concept of *ātman*, an indescribable reality. Nāgārjuna's criticism would not be that the concept is false, but that it is unintelligible. In fact, Kant's position appears contradictory in that he sometimes admitted that we can know or infer the unknown noumenon.

The Mādhyamika critique of the scholastic Buddhist idea of *svabhāva*, own-existence, is the denial of anything self-existing, transcendent or noumenal. There is no room for Kant's noumenon in Nāgārjuna's argument for the emptiness of all things. Thus an appraisal of Mādhyamika emptiness as something transcendent which belongs to the Kantian sphere of noumenon seems misplaced.

Kant criticized metaphysical theories such as rational psychology, speculative cosmology and natural theology,[10] but he did not reject all metaphysical issues as meaningless problems. According to Kant, the term *God*, for instance, was not a nonsensical concept. One of the chief aims of his philosophy was the accommodation of belief in God. For Nāgārjuna, God is an unintelligible concept, hence it would make no sense to make room for belief in God. Philosophers should not engage themselves in finding a basis for theological beliefs.

Epistemologically, Kant's critical philosophy aimed to limit our intellectual activities to the sphere of experience. Our knowledge of things, according to Kant, should be restricted to empirical or phenomenal reality. Human categories or concepts can give men knowledge "only through their possible application to *empirical intuition*. In other words, they serve only for the possibility of *empirical knowledge*; and such knowledge is what we entitle experience."[11] In examining *a priori* principles of the understanding, Kant wrote, "The final outcome of this whole section is therefore this: all principles of the pure understanding are nothing more than principles *a priori* of the possibility of experience, and to experience alone do all *a priori* synthetic propositions relate—indeed, their possibility itself rests entirely on this relation."[12] For Kant, perception or empirical intuition is the chief source and means of empirical knowledge. As he put it, "directly or indirectly, all thinking must ultimately...refer to perception, and therefore, with us, to sensibility, because in no other way can an object be given to us."[13]

Nāgārjuna's rejection of the concept of noumena does not imply that he accepted the legitimate use of human categories or concepts in the realm of phenomena. From the Mādhyamika standpoint, empirical reality or the phenomenally real are unintelligible ideas. What is empirical or phenomenal is supposed to be causally dependent and hence is devoid of its own nature, but what is real must have its own nature or essence. The term *empirical reality*, as we have seen, would mean that that which lacks its own nature has its own nature, and to call something phenomenally real is tantamount to claiming that a thing without essential nature has essential nature. These are contradictions in terms.[14]

According to the Mādhyamikas, perception appears to be the chief basis of empirical judgment, but in reality cannot be intelligently established. Nāgārjuna pointed out that perception involves a perceiver and the act of perceiving. The concept of a perceiver, for him, was as untenable as *ātman*, and the act of perceiving impossible. If there is an act of perceiving, it must occur in that which is already perceived, in that which is being perceived, or in that which is yet to be perceived. But we cannot find any act of perceiving in that which is already perceived, because it has already been perceived. We cannot find an act of perceiving in that which is yet to be perceived because it is not yet. Nor can we find an act of perceiving in that which is being perceived since (as in Nāgārjuna's argument for the impossibility of motion) there can be that which is being perceived if and only if there is the act of perceiving. But we are still examining whether there is the act of perceiving, and cannot use that which is being perceived to establish the act.[15] Thus, since neither a perceiver nor an act of perceiving can be established, it makes no sense to hold that perception is the source and means of *a posteriori* judgments, or that objects of knowledge must be perceivable. Similarly, Kant's *a priori* form of perception would be considered nonsensical.

Nāgārjuna did not aim to limit the validity of reason or confine the intellect to the phenomenal sphere. In Mādhyamika terms, it is an attachment to make a commitment to either noumenon or phenomenon. Murti's observation, "The purpose of the [Mādhyamika] dialectic is to demonstrate the subjectivity of the categories of thought, namely, that they are of empirical validity and can be significantly used within phenomena only; the Noumenon (*tattva*) is transcendent to thought,"[16] seems inaccurate.

Philosophy, for Nāgārjuna, was neither the description of the noumenal nor that of the phenomenal. His dialectic aimed to show that the so-called "perception," "experience," "phenomenon," "noumenon," or other concepts which have been used by people to describe and explain the true nature of things, are really empty. But philosophers often fail to see the empty nature of those concepts and believe that they stand for something real in the world; consequently they are attached to something and multiply ontological entities beyond necessity. The difficulty and much philosophical reasoning, for Nāgārjuna, comes from the fact that words are thought to be intrinsically related to the things for which they stand. Words and concepts must stand for some thing. If we know, there must be some thing which we know. If we err, we must have made an error in some thing. Like many metaphysicians, Kant seemed liable to this way of thinking. He wrote, "Truth and error, therefore, and consequently also illusion as leading to error, are only to be found in the judgment, i.e. only in the relation of the object to our understanding. In any knowledge which completely accords with the laws of understanding there is no error."[17] Many contemporary Mādhyamika scholars have similar tendencies. Even the term *empty* or *emptiness* is thought to refer to some thing, whether absolute reality or nothingness. As we have seen, Nāgārjuna condemned both absolutism and nihilism by saying, "If there is a thing that is not empty, then there must be something that is empty. Since nothing is non-empty, how can there be an empty thing?"[18]

The conceptual way of thinking, according to San-lun masters, is a disease (*ping*).[19] If it is not cured, men will continue to be prone to look for some "thing" even though their intellectual reasoning is confined within the sphere of their experience. People are unsuspectingly led into speculating: Is this "something" one or many? Is it directly or indirectly perceived? Is it *a priori* or *a posteriori*? Is it subjective or objective? Unlike Kant,[20] Nāgārjuna was optimistic about the elimination of metaphysical speculation. According to San-lun Buddhists, the cure of the disease lies not so much in limiting intellectual research to the realm of the phenomenal and trying to answer those questions, as in ruling out those problems as conceptual confusions. "Emptiness" does not "stand for" or "refer to" anything, but is a soteriological device to cure the disease by showing that all things are empty. Linguistically, to see everything as empty is to abandon the assumption of a one-to-one correlation between concepts or categories and extra-linguistic referents. This makes one realize that metaphysical questions of the world are absurd, and hence frees one from metaphysical speculation.

II. Nāgārjuna and Wittgenstein on Language

Both before and at the time of Nāgārjuna,[21] most Indian philosophers agreed with the concept of meaning as a relation between words and objects.[22] If words do not correspond to objects, they are unreliable and false; only if they correspond are they reliable and true. There are two views on the nature of the objects to which words refer: one holds that the referent or object for which the word stands is particular, and the other holds that it is universal.[23] However, both are examples of a referential theory of meaning which claims, roughly, that the meaning of a word is an extra-linguistic object for which it stands and, consequently, that a word is meaningful only if it stands for an object. Words which stand for the same object have the same meaning.

The Mādhyamika doctrine of emptiness aimed to refute this popular approach. According to Nāgārjuna, words have no meaning of themselves, and the meaning of a term is not the object for which it stands, but depends on conditions or circumstances. If the conditions differ, the meaning of the word would be different and might even be lost. The Buddha might conform to the worldly linguistic usage and say that man enters *nirvāṇa*; the words seem to denote objects, and there seem to be a man and a place, *nirvāṇa*. From the standpoint of higher truth, there are no extra-linguistic realities such as man and the place of *nirvāṇa*. Nāgārjuna wrote, "Things are not attainable. Once all conceptualization or language ceases, there is no man and no place. So the Buddha does not say anything."[24]

Even the term *Tathāgata* has no meaning by itself; it is as empty as any other term we use to describe the world. One should not give a special ontic status to Tathāgata and be attached to it, for its ontic status is as incomprehensible and unintelligible as those of things we can find in the universe.[25] According to the Mādhyamikas, all words and names are merely conventional conveniences given due to human ignorance. Extra-linguistic realities or objects, even the Tathāgata, are subject to the same criticism as the concepts of *ātman* and *dharma*.[26] Extra-linguistic referents are not actual, but are projections of the human mind, objectified concepts. Nāgārjuna said simply, "Words have no essence. Whatever is expressed by them is also without essence."[27] In the *Chao-lun*, Seng-chao wrote:

> If you seek a thing through a name, in the thing there is no actual that matches the name. If you seek a name through a thing, the name has no efficacy to obtain the thing. A thing without an actual to match its name is not a thing. A name without efficacy to obtain a thing is not a name. Therefore, names do not match actuals, and actuals do not match names. Since there is no matching of names and actuals, where do the myriad things occur?[28]

According to the San-lun masters, language is like a fish-trap which can be used to attract sentient beings to the Buddha's *Dharma*. But the true meaning of the *Dharma* can be known only if one sees the emptiness of words and consequently discards language. In his preface to Nāgārjuna's *Twelve Gate Treatise*, Seng-jui (352-446) stated, "Only when our language (*ch'üan*, fish-trap) and the self are both forgotten can one realize the true meaning."[29] Out of compassion the Buddha might use language to explain and spread his *Dharma*. But as a skillful teacher, he used words and names without attributing any reality or own-being to them. The ultimate goal of his preaching was to give up preaching, and to help people to discard language and know truth without any conceptualization. Nāgārjuna concluded the *Middle Treatise* with these words: "I humbly offer reverence to Gautama who out of compassion taught this truth to abandon all discursive views."[30]

Nāgārjuna's philosophy of emptiness appears similar to Wittgenstein in that both considered language a tool. For both, the meaning of a word lies not in an object or referent but in context or circumstances. If the context changes, meaning changes. Both claim that metaphysical systems are fabrications that misconceive the role of language in relation to the world. According to Nāgārjuna and Wittgenstein, philosophy cannot be a factual science about the nature of things, and the philosophers' main business is not to explain the universe.

However, apparent similarities should not lead scholars to suggest, "There is not nearly as much difference between the roles of Wittgenstein and Nāgārjuna as one might imagine."[31] In fact, there are fundamental differences between the two. According to Wittgenstein, the referential view of meaning is erroneous but the contextual view is not. For him, "the meaning of a word is its use in the language.... Every sign *by itself* seems dead. What gives it life?... In use it is *alive*."[32] When men are looking for the meaning, they are tempted to look for some object which they might call "the meaning." In order to avoid this, Wittgenstein urged, "Don't ask for the meaning, ask for the use."[33]

Although he repudiated the metaphysical use of language, Wittgenstein acknowledged the validity of the everyday use of language. He did not think that there is any need to construct a new ideal language in order to clear away conceptual confusions. For him, "every sentence in our language 'is in order as it is.' That is to say, we are not *striving after* an ideal, as if our ordinary vague sentences had not yet gotten a quite unexceptionable sense, and a perfect language awaited construction by us.... On the other hand it seems clear that where there is sense there must be perfect order.... So there must be perfect order even in the vaguest sentence."[34] Wittgenstein did not question the function of predication in ordinary language. We can intelligently ascribe *true* or *false* to propositions. He wrote:

> Let us examine the proposition: "This is how things are."... How can I say that this is the general form of propositions?... It is first and foremost *itself* a proposition, an English sentence, for it has a subject and a predicate....
>
> At bottom, giving "This is how things are" as the general form of propositions is the same as giving the definition: A proposition is whatever can be true or false. For instead of "This is how things are" I could have said, "This is true." (Or again, "This is false.")[35]

His critique of metaphysics intends to change our use of language from a metaphysical to an ordinary use. He seemed to believe that if we confine our use of language to the ordinary one, philosophical problems will be resolved. He stated, "What *we* do is to bring words back from their metaphysical to their everyday use."[36] And: "The problems are solved, not by giving new information, but by arranging what we have already known."[37]

The philosopher's task is not to describe actual phenomena but to describe phenomena of language. Wittgenstein wrote, "Philosophy may in no way interfere with the actual use of language; it can in the end only describe it."[38]

From Nāgārjuna's standpoint, Wittgenstein's thinking would be dualistic. He made a division between meaning as an object and meaning as a use, metaphysical and ordinary uses, the description of non-linguistic facts and the description of linguistic facts, private language and public language, absolute and ordinary certainty.[39] For Wittgenstein, doubt makes sense only in terms of what is not doubtful.[40] He seemed committed to the view of meaning as use, the legitimacy of the ordinary use of language, the description of linguistic facts, the rationality of public language and the presupposition of ordinary certainty.[41] These, for the Mādhyamika, would be attachments, not necessarily better than the traditional attachments of metaphysicians.

According to the teaching of emptiness as the middle way, it is even erroneous to hold a contextual view of meaning. Wittgenstein aimed to show that the meaning of words is derived from the relationship which one linguistic unit has with others, while Nāgārjuna aimed to show that no legitimate relationship between linguistic units can be established. Language, according to Nāgārjuna, appears to have a legitimate function when seen from the conventional standpoint; yet again, if we really examine ordinary language use, we find that it involves contradiction. So it would make no sense to define the meaning of a word as its "use" or to insist that the meaning of words is derived from the relationship which one word has with other words.

Nāgārjuna critically examined the structure of verbal expression and argued that the relationship between two basic linguistic units, the subject and the predicate, cannot be rationally established, and that predication in ordinary use of language is really unintelligible. He asked, "What is the precise relationship between the subject and the predicate?" "Is the subject identical with or different from the predicate?" If the subject is the same as the predicate, they would be one and it would make no sense to call one a subject and the other a predicate. Actually, if the subject and predicate were identical, the sentence would be a tautology. It would say nothing about the world and hence there would not be a real functioning of predication. If on the other hand, the subject is different from the predicate, there would be no particular connection between them. How can we say that the latter is predicated of the former? And also, if the subject and the predicate differ, how can two "different" linguistic units make "one" sentence and describe the "same" state of affairs?[42]

Further, when we use ordinary language in an expression or sentence, we relate or ascribe a predicate to a subject. Nāgārjuna asked, what is the status of subject before predication? Does it already have other predicates predicated of it or not? If the subject does not have any other predicate predicated of it, how can this be the case? Because if a subject is without any predicate predicated of it, it is incomprehensible and nonexistent. If a subject without a predicate is nonexistent, to what does our predicate apply? If on the other hand, the subject does have some other predicate predicated of it before we ascribe a predicate, what further function would be served by ascribing an additional predicate since it already has something predicated of it? If it needs this predicate, a second and a third can in principle be applied. This would lead to an infinite regress. So Nāgārjuna came to the conclusion:

> There is no functioning of predication either in the case where a subject has some other predicate predicated of it or in the case where a subject does not have some other predicate predicated of it. And there is no functioning of predication in any other case besides these two cases. [Therefore predication in language is really impossible.][43]

Thus, unlike Wittgenstein, Nāgārjuna questioned the rationality and validity of the everyday use of language and contended that predication in our language cannot be established. Since there cannot be any function of predication, it makes no sense to find "use" or "function" of words or sentences, or to claim that the meaning of a word or sentences is its "use" in language.

From Nāgārjuna's standpoint, the view that "the meaning of a word is its use in the language" really involves a contradiction or absurdity. Wittgenstein's thesis indicates that the meaning of a word is "fixed" or "determined" by its particular use in the particular situation.[44] This implies that each word has its own or particular use in the language and that that particular use is its meaning. But language, Nāgārjuna might point out, is an organized system of signs where words are inter-related and hence are devoid of their own uses. So, the thesis that the meaning of a word is its use in the language would be to say that a word has its own use in an organized system of signs where every word is devoid of its own use. This is contradictory.

Since the function of predication and a meaningful concept of use in language cannot be established, from Nāgārjuna's perspective it is nonsensical to confine philosophical research to a description of how language "works" or "functions." Philosophers, for Nāgārjuna, should not waste their time in describing the actual use or phenomena of language. His teaching of emptiness as the middle way would warn: Don't ask for the meaning; don't ask for the use either. It would also warn: Attempt neither to explain extra-linguistic reality nor to describe linguistic phenomena. One should rather know that all things are empty. To know that all things are empty is to see that all conceptualizations involve contradictions or absurdities and hence ought to be eliminated. "In *Śūnyatā*," Nāgārjuna wrote, "one gives up playing the language game (*hsi-lun*) or conceptualization."[45] Chi-tsang stated:

> It is not that language is given in order to have philosophy (or teaching), but rather that philosophy is presented in order to eliminate language.[46]

Although both Nāgārjuna and Wittgenstein refuted metaphysical assertions as conceptual confusions, they did this in different ways and for different reasons. According to Nāgārjuna, the trouble with metaphysical inferences does not merely come from the fact that metaphysicians go beyond the legitimate use of language, but also from the fact that language itself is inadequate and unintelligible. The problem lies not so much in the misuse of language, as in the impossibility of the intelligent use of language. To change the metaphysical use of language to an ordinary use cannot solve all philosophical problems. The complete solution, for Nāgārjuna, lies in the abandonment of conceptualization. Nāgārjuna tried to achieve this by means of a dialectic in the form of *reductio ad absurdum*. This type of dialectic does not play an important role in Wittgenstein's philosophy, although he rejected private language on the ground that it involves contradictions. Unlike Wittgenstein, Nāgārjuna exercised his dialectic to criticize even public language.

From Nāgārjuna's Buddhist standpoint, Wittgenstein would be attached to the ordinary use of public language, and his philosophy incomplete. Although he recognized the inadequacy of metaphysical language, he was still bound by conceptualization. Not being so bound, according to San-lun masters, gave Nāgārjuna and his followers freedom for creativity. True Mādhyamikas are free to apply any means to express enlightenment and help others obtain *nirvāṇa*. They may apply an ordinary statement to refute a metaphysical assertion, or call on metaphysics to refute ordinary statements. They may not use language, may keep silent, may use strange words or gestures to communicate. Seng-chao observed, "Therefore the sage always speaks and never speaks. Now I will attempt with crazy words to explain it (*prajñā*) to you."[47]

This kind of freedom and creativity was exemplified by Zen Buddhism in their "paradoxical words and strange actions" (*chi-yen-chi-hsing*). Perhaps San-lun masters would say that, for the sake of this freedom, Wittgensteinians should become Mādhyamikas. As an adherent of Mādhyamika Buddhism, San-lun Buddhists might claim, one would at least have a more complete analysis of language.

Notes

Preface

1. M. Hiriyanna, *Outlines of Indian Philosophy* (London: Allen and Unwin, 1932), p. 206.

2. Chris Gudmunsen, *Wittgenstein and Buddhism* (New York: Barnes and Noble, 1977), p. viii.

3. The *Chung-lun* was translated by Kumārajīva in A.D. 409 from the now lost *Mādhyamika-śāstra*. The main verses were given by Nāgārjuna, and its commentary was provided by Piṅgala. This treatise exists only in Chinese. The *Shih-erh-men-lun* was also translated by Kumārajīva in A.D. 408-9 from the now lost *Dvādasa-dvāra-śāstra*. Both main verses and commentary were given by Nāgārjuna. It does not exist in the Sanskrit original nor in the Tibetan translation. The *Pai-lun* was translated by Kumārajīva in A.D. 404 from the *Śata-śāstra*. Its main verses were given by Āryadeva and its commentary was given by Vasu.

121

Chapter One

General Introduction

1. The term Śākyamuni means the sage or holy man of the Śākyas. For the life of Śākyamuni, see E.J. Thomas, *The Life of the Buddha as Legend and History* (London: Kegan Paul, 1949), Wm. Theodore de Bary, ed.; *The Buddhist Tradition in India, China and Japan* (New York: Modern Library, 1969), pp. 55-72; and Aśvaghosha, *Buddhacarita*, ed. by E.H. Johnston (Calcutta: Baptist Mission Press, 1935).

2. Siddhartha in Pāli. It means "he who has achieved his goal."

3. A chiseled inscription on a stone pillar unearthed around the turn of the century in the northern Indian hamlet of Rummindei (Lumbini, which was recently renamed Lumbani, after the area was reverted to the Nepalese government by the British during the decolonization process), identifies it as the place of birth of Siddhārtha Gautama. The pillar was situated there by the order of King Aśoka (270-237 or 236 B.C.).

4. The word *dharma* in Buddhism has many different

meanings. It can mean truth, law, norm, doctrine, teaching, sermon, righteousness, according to the context. Phenomena in general are *dharma*, as are the qualities and characteristics of phenomena. When it is used with a capital letter, it means primarily Truth, Law, or Doctrine.

5. The word *saṅgha* literally means assembly, collection, company, or society. Here it means primarily the monastic order, the Buddhist church or community. Buddha, *Dharma* and *Saṅgha* are known as the Three Jewels in Buddhism. The Buddhist proclamation of allegiance for monk and layman is: "I take my refuge in the Buddha, I take my refuge in the *Dharma*, I take my refuge in the *Saṅgha*."

6. The life of the Buddha has been dated variously by modern scholars: 560-480 B.C., 563-483 B.C., or 559-478 B.C.

7. *Saṁyutta-nikāya*, II, 106; Anada K. Coomaraswamy, *Hinduism and Buddhism* (Westport, Connecticut: Greenwood Press, 1971), pp. 45-46.

8. The word *karma* literally means action, work, deed or product. It is used for the mysterious power which causes all action to work itself out in requital in another life. It is also the moral action which causes further retribution, and either good or evil transmigration.

9. According to Brāhmanism, *ātman* is something permanent and eternal. It can be known by intuition. But the Buddha is reported to have said, "Whatever is seen, heard, reflected, known, attained, searched for and contemplated upon by mind—that also is not mine, not the 'I,' and not my self." (*Majjhima-nikāya*, II, 136.)

10. For a comparative study of Buddhism and Hinduism, see

Kashi Nath Upadhyaya's *Early Buddhism and the Bhaga-vadgītā* (Delhi: Motilal Banarsidass, 1971). See also *Buddhism* and *Hinduism* by G. Upadhyaya (Banaras Hindu University Publication) and *Vedānta and Buddhism* by H. von Glasenapp (Kandy, Ceylon: Wheel Publication, 1958).

11. During the late fourth century B.C., the Buddhist organization was divided into two schools: the Mahāsaṅgika (the majority or great assembly) and the Sthaviras (the school of elders). Soon afterwards, during the third century B.C., some eight schools of dissenters arose from the Mahāsaṅgika. During the second and third centuries B.C., some ten schools of dissenters arose from the Sthaviras. These eighteen schools were later referred to as Hīnayāna. The traditions surrounding these schools are unreliable, contradictory and confused. See Edward Conze's *Buddhist Thought in India* (Ann Arbor: University of Michigan Press, 1967), pp. 119-120.

12. The Pāli canon was compiled and edited by three monastic councils. The First Council assembled just a few months after the death of Buddha (483 B.C.) in Rājagaha, the Second about a hundred years later (around 383 B.C.) in Vesālī, and the Third in 225 B.C. in Pātaliputra. The canon is divided into three collections called "Baskets" (*piṭaka*). The first collection, the *Vinayapiṭaka*, contains the rules for monastic discipline (*vinaya*), the second, the *Suttapiṭaka*, the sermons (*sutta*) of the Buddha and his disciples, and the third, the *Abhidhammapiṭaka*, the codifications and analyses of the teachings. There are certain extra-canonical Pāli works such as the *Milindapañha*, the *Visuddhimagga* and the scholastic manual *Abhidhammatthasaṅgaha*. The Sarvāstivāda scriptures were written in Sanskrit.

13. The word *arhat* means worthy or venerable. It refers to an

enlightened, saintly man for whom there will be no rebirth and who will enter into *nirvāṇa* after death.

14. There is no canon of the Mahāyāna because the Mahāyāna represents no unity of sects. There are only separate *sūtras* which are called Mahāyāna *sūtras*, originally written in Sanskrit. Many of these Sanskrit originals have been lost, and are preserved mainly in their Chinese and Tibetan translations. The earlist Māhāyana literature is the *Prajñā* or "wisdom" literature. It consists of a huge body of texts whose composition is spread over a thousand years. The basic text is the *Perfection of Wisdom in 8,000 Lines*, which was composed about 100 B.C. by an unknown author or authors. About the beginning of the Christian era, the Wisdom text was expanded, the longest to 100,000 lines. Around 300-500 the texts were shortened; the best products of this process are the *Heart Sūtra* and the *Diamond Cutter Sūtra*. There are many individual Mahāyāna *sūtras* that serve as the main texts of particular Mahāyāna schools. For example, the *Lotus of the Good Law* (*Saddharmapuṇḍari-ka*) is the basic scripture of the T'ien-t'ai School. The Hua-yen School has as its main text the *Garland Sūtra* (*Avataṁ-saka*). The teaching of the Pure Land School is based upon the *Pure Land Sūtra* (*Sukhāvativyūha*). Other Mahāyāna scriptures are too numerous to mention.

15. The term *bodhisattva* literally means "being of wisdom." It was first used in the sense of a previous incarnation of the Buddha. Many lives before his final birth as Siddhārtha Gautama the Bodhisattva did mighty deeds of compassion and self-sacrifice, as he gradually perfected himself in wisdom and virtue.

16. They believed that their teachings were the orthodox and original form of Buddhism.

17. *Majjhima-nikāya*, 63; Henry Clarke Warren, *Buddhism in Translation* (New York: Atheneum, 1970), pp. 117-122.

18. See Rhys Davids, *Dialogues of the Buddha* (Sacred Books of the Buddhist series), I, pp. 187-188.

19. Warren, *op. cit.*, p. 126.

20. *Sutta-nipāta*, ed. by D. Anderson and H. Smith (London: Pali Text Society, 1913), 781.

21. Rhys Davids, *op. cit.*

22. *Ibid.*

23. It should be noted that Pure Land Buddhism does hold that one obtains salvation not by his own effort, but by the compassion of Amita Buddha.

24. *Saṁyutta-nikāya*, III, 28; Kashi Nath Upadhyaya, *op. cit.*, p. 159.

25. The Vaibhāṣika School is a later appellation of the philosophy of the Sarvāstivāda School. The main philosophical work of the school is Katyaniputra's *Ābhidharmajñāna-prasthāna-śāstra* composed in the second century B.C. The next work of the school was *Ābhidharmamahāvibhāsā-śāstra* or simply *Vibhāṣā* composed at the council of Kaniska about 78. It was from this text that the name Vaibhāṣika was derived. *Vibhāṣā* is a commentary and the philosophy has been so called because it was based on the commentaries rather than on the original texts of the teachings of the Buddha.

26. The Sautrāntikas are those who hold the *sūtras* as their

authority and not the *śāstra*. They do not admit the authority of the *Abhidharma* of the Sarvāstivādins. The text on which this school is based belonged to the Ārya Sthaviras and possibly to the Mahāsaṅghikas. The main philosophical principles of the school are said to have been formulated by Dharmottara in Kashmir about 78, but according to Hsüan-tsang it was founded by the famous teacher Kumāralabdha.

27. F.Th. Stcherbatsky, *Buddhist Logic* (New York: Dover, 1962), Vol. I, p. 225; see also T.R.V. Murti, *The Central Philosophy of Buddhism* (London: Allen and Unwin, 1970), pp. 81-82.

28. John Locke, *An Essay Concerning Human Understanding*, 2, 8, 8.

29. See Richard I. Aaron, *John Locke* (Oxford: Clarendon Press, 1965), pp. 99-115.

30. According to scholars such as David J. Kalupahana, the Buddhist thought in the Pali Nikāyas and the Chinese Āgamas, which may represent the earliest sources for the study of Buddhism (their collection and arrangement took place during the first hundred and fifty years after the death of the Buddha), is different from the Abhidharma philosophy. The former is empiricistic and antimetaphysical and the latter, transcendentalistic and metaphysical. For a detailed discussion of Kalupahana's viewpoint, see his book, *Buddhist Philosophy: A Historical Analysis* (Honolulu: University Press of Hawaii, 1976).

31. See Shoson Miyamoto, "Voidness and the Middle Way," *Studies on Buddhism in Japan* (Tokyo, 1939), I, p. 88. See also Hajime Nakamura, *A Critical Survey of Indian Reli-*

gions and Philosophy Chiefly Based upon Japanese Studies
(A Temporary Edition) (Hawaii, 1962), Chapter VII, 20.

32. They were supposed to have made contributions to the
development of the six traditional Indian schools of philosophy. See Wm. Theodore de Barry, ed., *Sources of Indian
Tradition* (New York: Columbia University Press, 1958), p.
158. See also F. Stcherbatsky, *The Concept of Buddhist
Nirvāṇa* (Leningrad: Office of the Academy of Sciences of
the U.S.S.R., 1927), p. 62; and K.P. Jayaswal and Rahula
Sankrityayana, eds., "Vigrahavyāvartanī by Achārya
Nāgārjuna: With the Author's Own Commentary," *Journal
of the Bihar and Orissa Research Society*, XXIII (Part III,
1937), vii.

33. The word *dharma* (*fa*) has been used in several different
ways by the Buddhists. Generally speaking, it has the following meanings:
   (1) *Dharma* as conceived by the Buddha in meditation
       means perfect enlightenment and perfect wisdom.
   (2) *Dharma* as expressed in words and speech means the
       Buddha's sermon, teaching, dialogue, doctrine, sacred
       text and doctrinal text.
   (3) *Dharma* as set forth for his disciples means discipline,
       rule, precept, regulation of conduct and morality.
   (4) *Dharma* as being the object of knowing means truth,
       theory, principle, law and knowledge.
   (5) *Dharma* as being the reality of the universe means thing,
       fact, element, factor, existence, constituent of our
       experience, and truly real event.
   (6) *Dharma* as being the objective data of reality means
       characteristic, mark, attribute and quality.

In the realistic philosophy of the Abhidharma Buddhists the
word *dharma* is applied mostly in the context of (5) and (6):

it is used to explain and describe the true nature of the universe.

34. The *Middle Treatise*, XV: 1-2.

35. See the *Twelve Gate Treatise*, IX-XII.

36. 1. The first pair involved the reality of objects in the universe. The eternalists held that everything exists, but the annihilists contended that nothing exists. According to the Buddha, both of them were extreme views. He avoided them by proclaiming the doctrine of perpetual flux (*anicca*).

2. The second pair of extremes was the fatalistic and the fortuitist theories. The former claimed that all things are predetermined, while the latter argued that everything happens by chance without a cause or condition. The Buddha refuted them by teaching the doctrine of dependent origination (*paṭiccasamutppāda*) according to which the existence of everything is conditional and dependent on a cause or causes, and nothing occurs fortuitously.

3. The third pair outlined moral responsibility and human actions. According to Kriyāvāda, all pleasures and sufferings are due to our own efforts, and we should be responsible for whatever we do. But according to Akriyāvāda, we should not be responsible for our actions because pleasures and sufferings are due to other factors and man has no role to play in them. The Buddha maintained the middle way by teaching that the *Vedanā* depends partly on ourselves and partly on other factors.

4. Finally, the Buddha's middle way refuted hedonism and asceticism. The materialists revel in sensual pleasures and live a hedonistic way of life. The traditional religious men, on the other hand, avoided any sense pleasure and mortified their bodies. For the Buddha, both ways were

extremes. He avoided them by preaching the Eightfold Noble Path.

See Kashi Nath Upadhyaya, *op. cit.*, pp. 90-91; see also Jayatilleke's *Early Buddhist Theory of Knowledge* (London: Allen & Unwin, 1963), pp. 359-360.

37. See Luis O. Gomez, "Proto-Mādhyamika in the Pāli Canon," *Philosophy East and West*, Vol. 26, No. 2 (April 1976), pp. 137-165.

38. The *Prajñāparamitā* literature, which is preserved in Sanskrit, Chinese and Tibetan, consists of a huge body of texts composed for over more than a thousand years. Generally speaking, its composition can be divided into four periods: (1) *c.* 100 B.C.-100 A.D., composition of basic texts; (2) *c.* 100 A.D.-300, expansion of basic texts; (3) *c.* 300-500, restatement of teachings in shorter *sūtras*; and (4) *c.* 500-1200, composition of commentaries and Tantric influence.

39. See D.T. Suzuki, *Studies in the Laṅdkāvatāra Sūtra* (London: Routledge and Kegan Paul Ltd., 1972), p. 95.

40. The *Aṣṭasāhasrikā*, Chapter II, p. 34; D.T. Suzuki, *Ibid.*

41. See Chandradhar Sharma, *Indian Philosophy: A Critical Survey* (London, 1962), pp. 72-73, and *Dialectic in Buddhism and Vedānta* (Banaras, 1952). See also A. Berriedal Keith, *Buddhist Philosophy in India and Ceylon* (Oxford: The Clarendon Press, 1923), p. 230, and H.N. Randle, *Indian Logic in the Early Schools* (London, 1930), pp. 17-18.

42. This point was well discussed by Y. Sogen in his *Systems of Buddhistic Thought*.

43. For them, mind is divided into eight areas of consciousness: in addition to six kinds of *vijñānas*, which are known to the Sarvāstivādin school, *caksu* (the eye), *srotra* (the ear), *ghrāṇa* (the nose), *jihvā* (the tongue), *kāya* (the sense of touch), and *māna* (the sense center), they add *mano-vijñāna* (the thought center) and *ālaya-vijñāna*. The *ālaya-vijñāna* is the main substratum of transmigration in *saṁsāra* (the wheel of life and death), yet it is not an unchanging substance like the soul or *ātman*, but rather a stream of continuously changing states. Also for the Yogācāra, pain or pleasure, good or evil, right or wrong are merely the outward development of potential seeds which are stored in the *ālava-vijñāna*, the store-house-consciousness. There are two kinds of potential seeds: the seed which is full of defilement and the seed which is free from defilement. The first seed is comprised of the first two principles of the four noble truths: life in this world is full of suffering and there is a cause of this suffering. This seed can give rise to the thoughts, desires, and attachments which increasingly bind us to the fictitious and imaginary phenomenal world. The second seed represents the last two principles of the four noble truths: it is possible to stop suffering and there is a path which leads to the cessation of suffering. Through self-control, this second seed can gradually stop the rise of undesirable mental states and develop the ideal state of *nirvāṇa*. In the *ālaya-vijñāna* there is stored a twofold seed from which springs up the *saṁsāra* and the *nirvāṇa*. All is ideal.

44. Sogen, *op. cit.*, p. 229.

45. For the English version of this treatise, see Hsueh-li Cheng's *Nāgārjuna's Twelve Gate Treatise* (Boston: D. Reidel Publishing Company, 1982).

Chapter Two

Principle Mādhyamika Doctrines

1. Shōson Miyamoto, "The Buddha's First Sermon and the Original Patterns of the Middle Way," *Indogaku Bukkyōgaku Kenkyū*, Vol. 13, No. 2 (1965), pp. 885-845; "Voidness and Middle Way," *Studies on Buddhism In Japan*, vol. 1, pp. 73-92.

2. T.R.V. Murti, "Saṁvṛti and Paramārtha in Mādhyamika and Advaita Vedānta," in *The Problem of Two Truths in Buddhism and Vedānta*, ed. by Mervyn Sprung (Boston: D. Reidel Publishing Company, 1973), pp. 9-26.

3. Mervyn Sprung, "The Mādhyamika Doctrine of Two Realities as a Metaphysic," *Ibid.*, pp. 40-53. See also David J. Kalupahana, *op. cit.*, pp. 134-137.

4. Edward Conze, *Buddhist Thought in India*, pp. 239-243. See also David J. Kalupahana, *Ibid.*, pp. 132-139.

5. Wm. Theodore de Bary, *The Buddhist Tradition in India, China and Japan*, p. 71; it was translated from the *Buddhacarita*, Sanskrit text as ed. by E.H. Johnson, pp. 140-142.

6. *Ibid.*

7. As pointed out in the previous chapter, early Buddhists had developed several versions of the doctrine of the middle way. According to Stcherbatsky, Hīnayānists often held that the middle way is "between 'everything exists and nothing exists,' meaning that a limited catalogue of ultimate elements (*dharma*) exists in interdependent origination." *The Conception of Buddhist Nirvāṇa*, p. 81 n. See also Shoson Miyamoto, "A Re-appraisal of Pratityasamut-pāda," *Studies in Indology and Buddhology, Presented in Honor of Professor Susumu Yamaguchi on the Occasion of his Sixtieth Birthday* (Kyoto, 1955), pp. 156-157.

8. *Chu-shuo chung ti-i* can also mean (1) the foremost of all teachings, that is the Buddha's teaching; or (2) his teaching has to be grasped from the higher perspective.

9. "*Yin-yüan*" can mean (1) that events are causally dependent upon each other; or (2) that concepts are dependent upon one another, that is, the meanings of all concepts are dependent on one another.

10. "*Shan-mieh chu hsi-lun*" can mean (1) that one should be good at getting rid of conceptualization or verbal expression or (2) one should be smart enough to eliminate conceptualization or verbal expression.

11. This is the opening statement of the *Middle Treatise*.

12. Junjirō Takakusu has a valuable observation on this: "The fact that there are just eight negations has no special purport: This is meant to be a wholesale negation. It may be taken as crosswise sweeping away of all eight errors attached to the world of becoming, or reciprocal rejection of

the four pairs of one-sided views, or a lengthwise general thrusting aside of the errors one after the other—for instance, refuting the idea of appearing (birth) by the idea of disappearance; the idea of motion hither by the idea of motion thither; this last idea by idea of permanence; permanence by destruction (end); destruction by unity; unity by diversity; diversity by appearance; and so on." *The Essentials of Buddhist Philosophy* (Honolulu: University Press of Hawaii, 1947), pp. 103-104.

13. See Satkari Mookerjee, *The Buddhist Philosophy of Universal Flux* (Delhi: Motilal Banarsidass, 1975), pp. 403-404. See also T.R.V. Murti, The Central Philosophy of Buddhism, pp. 131-132; R. Puligandla, "How Does Nāgārjuna Establish the Relativity of All Views?" *The Maha Bodhi*, Vol. 81, No. 5-6 (May-June 1973), p. 160.

14. The Mādhyamika seems to maintain that "the logic of common life is sufficient for showing that all systems contradict one another"; Stcherbatsky, *op. cit.*, p. 38n.; Murti, *Ibid.*, pp. 140, 144-146.

15. The *Middle Treatise*, XVII: 12a.

16. *Ibid.*, XXIII: 1a.

17. The *Middle Treatise*, XIII: 9a.

18. *Ibid.*, XXIV: the *Hui-cheng-lun*, 72.

19. For detailed discussions of this, see Bimal Krishna Matilal, *Epistemology, Logic, and Grammar In Indian Philosophical Analysis* (Paris: Mouton, 1971), pp. 148-151; "A Critique of the Mādhyamika Position," *The Problem of Two Truths*, ed. by Mervyn Sprung, pp. 56-57.

20. Seng-chao, *Chao-lun*, Part II, p. 152c.

21. The *Middle Treatise*, XVIII: 7.

22. *Ibid.*, XXIV: 8; the *Twelve Gate Treatise*, VIII. See Chi-tsang, *The Meaning of the Twofold Truth*, pp. 77-115, and *The Profound Meaning of The Treatises*, pp. 1-14.

23. For a detailed discussion of this, see Mervyn Sprung, ed., *op. cit.*, pp. 17, 38, 43 and 57, and N. Dutt, *Aspects of Mahāyāna Buddhism and Its Relation to Hīnayāna* (London, 1930), pp. 216-17.

24. For a detailed discussion, see Chi-tsang, *op. cit.* See also Mervyn Sprung, *Ibid.*, pp. 17, 43 and 58.

25. The *Middle Treatise*, XXIV: 9; the *Twelve Gate Treatise*, VIII.

26. Chi-tsang, *op. cit.*

27. The *Middle Treatise*, v: 8, and XIV: 7-9; the *Twelve Gate Treatise*, VIII.

28. H. Kern, *Manual of Indian Philosophy* (Strassburg: K.J. Trubner, 1896), p. 126.

29. A.B. Keith, *op. cit.*, p. 235.

30. *Ibid.*, p. 261.

31. Harsh Narain, "Śūnyavāda: A Reinterpretation" in *Philosophy East and West*, XIII, 4 (January, 1964), p. 311.

32. The *Middle Treatise*, XIV: 8; the *Twelve Gate Treatise*, VIII.

33. The four fruits of the *śramana* are the progressive achievements of the one who takes up the Buddhist principles (*srota-āpanna*), of the once-returner to the empirical level (*sakṛdāgāmin*), of the non-returner (*anāgāmin*), and of the enlightened worthy one (*arhat*).

34. The *Middle Treatise*, XXIV: 30.

35. *Ibid.*, XXIV: 32.

36. *Ibid.*, XXIV: 14; the *Twelve Gate Treatise*, VIII.

37. T.R.V. Murti, "Saṁvṛti and Paramārtha in Mādhyamika and Adaita Vedānta," *The Problem of Two Truths in Buddhism and Vedānta*, p. 22.

38. The *Middle Treatise*, XIII: 8. Nāgārjuna also said: "Nothing could be asserted to be *śūnya*, *aśūnya*, both *śūnya* and *aśūnya*, or neither *śūnya* nor *aśūnya*. They are stated as provisionary names." *Ibid.*, XXII: 11.

39. *Ibid.*, XIII: 8-9.

40. *Ibid.*, XXIV: 10; the *Twelve Gate Treatise*, VIII.

41. The *Twelve Gate Treatise*, VIII. Chi-tsang commented that "to know ultimate truth is to benefit oneself (self-interest); to know conventional truth is to be able to benefit others (other-interest); to know both truths simultaneously is to be able to benefit all equally (common-interest). Therefore it establishes the twofold truth." *A Commentary on the Twelve Gate Treatise*, (T1825), p. 206. See also *The Profound Meaning of Three Treatises*, p. 11, and *The Meaning of the Twofold Truth*, pp. 81, 82c, 85c and 86.

42. Chi-tsang, *The Meaning of the Twofold Truth*, pp. 79c and 81c.

43. Chi-tsang, *Ibid.*, p. 101

44. *Ibid.*, pp. 79, 95, 101, 102 and 112; see also *The Profound Meaning of Three Treatises*, pp. 3-11.

45. *Ibid.*, p. 98.

46. *Ibid.*, p. 95.

47. *Ibid.*, pp. 88c, 94, 107, 108, 109 and 114b.

48. *Ibid.*, pp. 83a, 107c and 114.

49. *Ibid.*, p. 81.

50. *Ibid.*, pp. 105a, 108c and 109.

51. *Ibid.*, pp. 104b and 107a.

52. Chi-tsang, *The Profound Meaning of Three Treatises*, p. 6.

53. *Ibid.*

54. See Bimal Krishna Matilal, *Epistemology, Logic and Grammar In Indian Philosophical Analysis*, pp. 162-165.

55. The *Hui-cheng-lun*, 24.

56. For this famous negative statement, see the *Bṛhadāraṇyaka Upaniṣad*, II, 3, 6; IV, 9, 26; IV, 2, 4; IV, 4, 22; IV, 5, 5.

57. S. Radhakrishnan, *Indian Philosophy* (London: George Allen and Unwin, 1927), Vol. 1, p. 662.

58. D.T. Suzuki, *Outlines of Mahayana Buddhism* (New York: Schocken Books, 1963), pp. 102-103. See also Ryotai Hatani, "Dialectics of the Mādhyamika Philosophy" in *Studies on Buddhism In Japan*, ed., by The International Buddhist Society (Tokyo, 1939), pp. 55 and 71; H.N. Chatterjee, *Mūla-Mādhyamika-Kārika of Nāgārjuna* (Calcutta: Sanskrit College, 1957), pp. XXIV and XXVIII.

59. See Frederick J. Streng, *Emptiness: A Study in Religious Meaning* (New York: Abingdon Press, 1967), pp. 146 and 162.

60. Chi-tsang, *The Profound Meaning of Three Treatises*, p. 6.

61. *Ibid.*

62. *Ibid.*, p. 7. This quotation was taken from Chapter One of the *Lotus Scripture* (*Saddharmapuṇḍarika Sūtra*).

63. *Ibid.*

64. Chi-tsang, *The Meaning of the Twofold Truth*, pp. 90-91.

65. Chi-tsang, *The Profound Meaning of Three Treatises*, p. 10.

66. "*Svabhāv*ically construed" means that being or non-being is each regarded as something possessing its own nature.

67. Chi-tsang, *Ibid.*, p. 11.

68. The *Middle Treatise*, XVIII: 5.

69. Hsueh-li Cheng, *op. cit.*, pp. 13-14.

Chapter Three

Mādhyamika and Zen

1. See Chang Chung-yuan, *Original Teachings of Ch'an Buddhism* (New York: Vintage Books, 1971), pp. 4-5, 10 and 43. See also Heinrich Dumoulin, *A History of Zen Buddhism* (New York: Pantheon Books, 1963), pp. 70, 81 and 117; Garma C.C. Chang, *The Practice of Zen* (New York: Harper & Row, 1970), pp. 171-4. Chang Chung-yuan wrote: "The real meaning of *śūnyatā*, or *k'ung*, is ontological. It is the absolute reality...." *Ibid.*, p. 43.

2. See D.T. Suzuki, *An Introduction to Zen Buddhism* (New York: Grove Press, 1964), pp. 58-65.

3. See Junjiro Takakusu, the *Essentials of Buddhist Philosophy* p. 159; see also D.T. Suzuki, *Zen Buddhism* (New York: Doubleday, 1956), ed. by William Barrett, p. 64.

4. *Sūtra Spoken by the Sixth Patriarch on the High Seat of the Treasure of the Law* (also called *The Sūtra of Hui-neng*), trans. from the Chinese into English by Wong Mou-lan (Hong Kong: H.K. Buddhist Book Distributor Press, 1952), p. 18.

5. Heinrich Dumoulin, *The Development of Chinese Zen* (New York: The First Zen Institute of America Inc., 1953), trans. from the German with additional notes and appendices by Ruth Fuller Sasaki, pp. 10, 53-55.

6. D.T. Suzuki, *An Introduction to Zen Buddhism*, p. 57. See also Heinrich Dumoulin, *Ibid.*, pp. 11, 55 and 57.

7. Garma C.C. Chang, *op. cit.*, p. 86.

8. Huang-po said, "If you can only rid yourselves of conceptual thought, you will have accomplished everything. But if you students of the Way do not rid yourselves of conceptual thought in a flash, even though you strive for aeon after aeon, you will never accomplish it." John Blofeld, *The Zen Teaching of Huang Po* (New York: Grove Press, 1958), p. 33.

9. Wm. Theodore de Bary, *The Buddhist Tradition in India, China and Japan*, p. 219.

10. Chang Chung-yuan, *op. cit.*, pp. 230-231.

11. See Hsueh-li Cheng, "The Problem of God in Buddhism," *The Theosophist*, Vol. 98, No. 9 (June, 1977), pp. 98-108.

12. *Ibid.*, pp. 102-105; see also Hsueh-il Cheng, "Nāgārjuna's Approach to the Problem of the Existence of God," *Religious Studies*, June 1976, No. 12, pp. 207-216.

13. D.T. Suzuki, *An Introduction to Zen Buddhism*, p. 40.

14. "What is the Buddha?" "A stick of dry dung." Garma C.C. Chang, *op. cit.*, p. 21.

15. "Who is the Buddha?" "Three pounds of flax." *Ibid.*, p. 71.

16. Chang Chung-yuan, *op. cit.*, p. 143.

17. *The Sūtra of Hui-neng*, p. 39.

18. *Ibid.*, p. 45.

19. Chang Chung-yuan, *op. cit.*, pp. 7 and 24.

20. Wm. Th. de Bary, *op. cit.*, p. 232.

21. Dumoulin, *op. cit.*, pp. 12 and 60.

22. Hui-neng is said to have claimed that he was illiterate; see *The Sūtra of Hui-neng*.

23. *Ibid.*, p. 33.

24. See *Ching-te-ch'uan-teng-lu* (Record of the Transmission of the Lamp); T 2076 in vol. 30. See also Chang Chung-yuan, *op. cit.*, pp. 189-190.

25. The *Twelve Gate Treatise*.

26. *Ibid.*, III and IV.

27. Heinrich Dumoulin, *op. cit.*, pp. 22-23.

28. *The Sūtra of Hui-neng*, p. 36.

29. Garma C.C. Chang, *op. cit.*, pp. 75-76.

30. Chang Chung-yuan, *op. cit.*, p. 139.

31. *Ibid.*, p. 197.

32. The *Twelve Gate Treatise*, X.

33. D.T. Suzuki, *op. cit.*, p. 61. See also Heinrich Dumoulin, *A History of Zen Buddhism*, p. 67.

34. *The Sūtra of Hui-neng*, p. 26.

35. *Ibid.*, pp. 6, 12 and 38.

36. *Ibid.*, p. 47.

37. *Ibid.*, p. 35. A monk, Ma-tsu, used to sit cross-legged all day meditating. His master, Nan-yueh Huai-jang (677-744), saw him and asked:
"What seekest thou here thus sitting cross-legged?"
"My desire is to become a Buddha."
Thereupon the master took up a piece of brick and began to polish it hard on the stone near by.
"What workest thou on so, my master?" asked Ma-tsu.
"I am trying to turn this into a mirror."
"No amount of polishing will make a mirror of the brick, sir."
"If so, no amount of sitting cross-legged as thou doest will make of thee a Buddha," said the master.
"What shall I have to do then?"
"It is like driving a cart; when it moveth not, wilt thou whip the cart or the ox?"
Ma-tsu made no answer.
The master continued: "Wilt thou practice this sitting cross-legged in order to attain *dhyāna* or to attain Buddhahood? If it is *dhyāna*, *dhyāna* does not consist in sitting or lying; if it is Buddhahood, the Buddha has no fixed forms. As he has no abiding place anywhere, no one can take hold of him, nor can he be let go. If thou seekest Buddhahood by thus sitting cross-legged, thou murderest him. So long as thou freest thyself not from sitting so, thou never comest to the truth." D.T. Suzuki, *Zen Buddhism*, pp. 89-90.

Chapter Four

The Mādhyamika Treatment
of Philosophical Issues

1. "*Jen-sheng hsi-lun, hsi-lun p'o hui-yen.*" The *Middle Treatise*, XXII: 15.

2. "*Shan-mieh chu hsi-lun.*" *Ibid.*, XXV: 24, XVIII: 5 and XVII: 24. It is interesting to see that "*hsi-lun*" means conceptualization, language, game or trick.

3. The *Middle Treatise*, XIII: 9.

4. Hīnayāna Buddhists, such as Vātsiputrīyas and Sāmmitīya, call it *pudgala*. They hold that "the person can be got at (*upalabhate*) as a reality in the ultimate sense (*paramatthena*), and it can become an object of true experience (*sacchikattha*)." See Edward Conze, *op. cit.*, p. 125.

5. The *Katha Upaniṣad* 2.8; see R.E. Hume, *The Thirteen Principal Upaniṣads* (London: Oxford University Press, 1921), p. 349.

6. The *Middle Treatise*, XXVII: 5, 6 and XVIII: 1a.

7. *Ibid.*, XXVII: 4, 7, XVIII: 1b and IX: 3, 5.

8. Āryaveda had a good discussion of this. See the *Hundred Treatise*, II, and the *Middle Treatise*, IX.

9. The *Middle Treatise*, XXVII: 8, XVIII: 6 and IX: 5. Thomas Silkstone has a good discussion of this point in his article "My Self and My World," *International Philosophical Quarterly*, Vol. 13 (September 1973), pp. 377-390.

10. Buddhist schools such as the Abhidharmakósa, the Mahāsanghika, the Mahisaśaka and the Sautrāntika hold that only the present is real. But the Sarvāstivādas maintain that the past, the present and the future are real.

11. The *skandhas* are the five constituents of a person, or self. (1) Form (*rūpa*) is the physical and material side of persons and things. (2) Sensations (*vedanā*) are pleasant, unpleasant and neutral feelings, experienced through the contact of physical and mental organs with the external world. (3) Perceptions (*saṁjñā*) recognize objects whether physical or mental. (4) Predispositions (*saṁskāra*) are tendencies, impulses and volitions generated by the impressions of past experience. What is generally known as *karma* comes under this group. (5) Consciousness (*vijñāna*) is awareness of the presence of some object. The aim of the *skandha* classification of things is to explain the true nature of phenomena without the substance or self. What we call a being, or an individual, or person is only a conventional name for the combination of these five aggregates. In providing an account of the origin of cognitions and the cognitive process, early Buddhists classify things into twelve *āyatanas*: six internal spheres or sense-organs (eye, ear, nose, tongue, body and mind), and six external spheres or sense-objects (visible form, sound, odor, taste, tangible things and mind-

objects such as ideas, thoughts and conceptions). Our visual and other cognitions occur when these internal and external spheres come together or when our sense-organs contact the sense-objects. And in providing an account of what physical objects are or what the ultimate components of existence are, early scholastic Buddhists also classify things into six or eighteen *dhātus*. According to the canons, the *dhātus* are six: earth, water, fire, air, space (or ether) and consciousness. The later and more popular version of the *dhātus* holds there are eighteen: the six sense-organs, the six sense-objects and the six corresponding sense-consciousnesses. The word *dhātus*, from *dha*, "to place," has several different meanings, but here it primarily means constituent, element or factor. The *dhātus* are the basic irreducible elements of which phenomenal things are composed.

12. For a discussion of the word *svabhāva*, see Richard H. Robinson, *The Buddhist Religion* (Belmont, Calif.: Dickerson Publishing Company, Inc., 1970), pp. 51-52.

13. The *Middle Treatise*, XV: 1-2.

14. *Ibid.*, VII: 23 and 25.

15. The *Twelve Gate Treatise*, VIII: 1.

16. In Chapter VII of the *Twelve Gate Treatise*, the opponent argues that at the beginning of change (or production) origination is used and hence there is origination. At the middle of change, duration is used and hence there is duration. At the end, cessation is used and hence there is cessation.

17. *Ibid.*

18. The *Middle Treatise*, VII: 2.

19. *Ibid.*, VII: 1; the *Twelve Gate Treatise*, IV: 2.

20. The *Twelve Gate Treatise*, VI: 1.

21. Frederick Copleston, *A History of Philosophy* (Garden City, N.Y.: Image Books), Vol. I, Part 1, p. 55. Heraclitus also says, "You cannot step twice into the same river, for fresh waters are ever flowing in upon you." *Ibid.*

22. *Ibid.*, pp. 73-76. The Eleatics hold that true being is to be found, not by sense but by thought, and thought shows that there can be no motion and no change.

23. Th. Stcherbatsky, *Buddhist Logic*, Vol. One (New York: Dover), p. 99.

24. The *Middle Treatise*, II: 1-21.

25. *Majjhima-nikāya*, I, 190-191.

26. Nāgārjuna said, "He who sees the *pratītyasamutpāda* can see the Buddha and [the teachings of] suffering, origination, cessation and the way." The *Middle Treatise*, XXIV: 40.

27. See Frederick J. Streng, "The Significance of *Pratītyasa-mutpāda* for Understanding the Relationship between *Samvṛti* and *Paramārthasatya* in Nāgārjuna." *The Problem of Two Truths in Buddhism and Vedānta*, pp. 27, 30 and 36.

28. See Walpola Rahula, *What the Buddha Taught* (New York: Grove Press, Inc., 1962), p. 53; *Majjhima-nikāya*, III (PTS edition), p. 63; *Samyutta-nikāya*, II (PTS edition), pp. 28 and 95.

29. This is called the general theory of causation. As moral law it is sometimes called the special theory of causation; see Th. Stcherbatsky, *Buddhist Logic*, Vol. I, p. 136.

30. The so-called four conditions are the following: (1) The cause condition. This acts as the chief cause, for example, the wind and water that cause the wave. (2) The sequential condition. This immediately follows a preceding condition, such as waves following one another. (3) The appropriating condition. This is the objective (or subjective) environment, like the basin or the boat. (4) The upheaving condition. This is that which brings all conditions to the climax, such as the last wave that upsets the boat.

   The twelve internal causal conditions can be stated as follows: (1) suffering, such as old age and death is due to (2) birth; which is due to (3) formation of being; which is due to (4) our mental clinging to objects; which is due to (5) thirst or desire for objects; which is due to (6) perception; which is due to (7) contact; which is due to (8) the six organs of senses; which are due to (9) name-form; and these cannot happen without (10) conscious mind; which is due to (11) the will to live; which is due to (12) ignorance.

31. Walpola Rahula, *op. cit.*, p. 54.

32. See David J. Kalupahana, *Causality: The Central Philosophy of Buddhism* (Honolulu: University of Hawaii Press, 1975), pp. 89-109.

33. Each relationship has four lemmas. Usually Nāgārjuna discussed only the first two lemmas; namely, "thesis" and "antithesis."

34. The *Middle Treatise*, XX: 1-4, 16-17; the *Twelve Gate Treatise*, I-III.

35. See the *Twelve Gate Treatise*, II. The same chapter includes several other arguments to refute the second view.

36. *Ibid.*

37. *Ibid.*

38. The *Middle Treatise*, XV: 1a.

39. *Ibid.*, XV: 2a.

40. *Ibid.*, XV: 2b.

41. *Ibid.*, XVII: 1-33.

42. *Ibid.*

43. The *Twelve Gate Treatise*, II.

44. The *Middle Treatise*, XXIV: 18; the *Hui-cheng-lun*, 72.

45. T.R.V. Murti, *op. cit.*, p. 226.

46. T.R.V. Murti, "*Saṁvṛti* and *Paramārtha* in Mādhyamika and Advaita Vedānta," in *The Problem of Two Truths in Buddhism and Vedānta*, p. 13.

47. Soon after the death of the Buddha many of his followers began to think of him as more than a human being. Hīnayānists showed a tendency to lift the Buddha, even during his early life, beyond the phenomenal into transcendental spheres. The Pāli texts show that the historical Śākyamuni

is not only above all ordinary mortals, but is the supreme deity (*devatideva*), who is omnipotent and omniscient. Mahāyānists such as Yogācāra and T'ien-t'ai Buddhists think of the Buddha as supramundane and even transcendent. The Buddha is spoken of as having a threefold body (*trikāya*): (1) *dharmakāya* or the ideal body whose nature is wisdom and principle; (2) *sambhogakāya* or enjoyment or the reward body which appears only for the *bodhisattvas*; and (3) *nirmānakāya* or the transformation body which manifests itself for ordinary persons for their worship. These *trikāya* are but three aspects of the one Buddha.

48. "Īśvara is not only *Śastrayoni*, but also the creator and sustainer of the intra-subjective (*vyāvahārika*) world common to all; the *jīvas* are the makers of the *pratibhāsika* world which is private and subjective. He is also the sustainer of the moral order." Murti, *The Central Philosophy of Buddhism*, p. 289n; see also L.R. Joshi, "A New Interpretation of Indian Atheism," *Philosophy East and West* (July, 1966), p. 190. Not all Indian people hold this view of Īśvara. For Advaita Vedāntism, Īśvara is *māyā* and only unenlightened persons would regard Īśvara as the omnipotent and omniscient creator, sustainer and destroyer of the world. See S.C. Chatterjee and D.M. Datta, *An Introduction to Indian Philosophy* (Calcutta: University of Calcutta, 1939), pp. 58-59.

49. See the *Twelve Gate Treatise*, X.

50. Nāgārjuna said, "The effect which has already been produced is not being produced; that which is not yet being produced is not produced. Without 'that which has already been produced' and 'that which is not yet produced,' 'that which is being produced' is not produced." *Ibid.*, Chapter XII: 1.

51. See Bertrand Russell and F.C. Copleston, "The Existence of God—A Debate," in *A Modern Introduction to Philosophy*, ed. by Paul Edwards and Arthur Pap (New York: Free Press, 1966), pp. 473-490. This debate was broadcast in 1948 on the Third Programme of the British Broadcasting Co.

David Hume seemed to talk about this too in *An Enquiry Concerning Human Understanding*, ed., L.A. Selby-Bigge (2nd, 1902), pp. 147f.

52. Russell, *op. cit.*, p. 479.

53. See the *Twelve Gate Treatise*, X.

54. Alfred Jules Ayer, *Language, Truth and Logic* (New York: Dover, 1946), p. 9.

55. Nāgārjuna did this in Chapter XXII of the *Middle Treatise*.

56. *Ibid.*, XXII: 15. For a detailed discussion of this, see Hsueh-li Cheng, "The Problem of God in Buddhism," *The Theosophist*, Vol. 98, No. 9 (June, 1977), pp. 98-108.

57. Alex Wayman, "Contributions to the Mādhyamika School of Buddhism," *Journal of the American Oriental Society*, vol. 89, No. 1 (1969), p. 148.

58. Kenneth K. Inada, *Nāgārjuna: Translation of His Mūlamadhyamaka-kārikā* with an Introductory Essay (Tokyo: The Hokuseido Press, 1970), p. 22.

59. Chi-tsang, *The Meaning of the Twofold Truth*, pp. 83a, 107c and 114.

60. *Ibid.*, p. 81.

61. *Ibid.*, pp. 104b and 107.

62. *Ibid.*, p. 95.

63. William James, *The Meaning of Truth* (Westport, Connecticut: Greenwood Press, 1971), p. 77.

64. William James, *Essays in Radical Empiricism* (New York, 1912), p. 253.

65. *Ibid.*, p. 255.

66. William James, *The Will to Believe and Other Essays* (New York, 1897), p. 11.

67. William James, *The Meaning of Truth*, pp. 5-6.

68. *Ibid.*, p. 195.

69. William James acknowledged the realities of relations as well as objects. He said, "Radical empiricism takes conjunctive relations at their face value, holding them to be as real as the terms united by them." *Essays in Radical Empiricism*, p. 107.

70. William James, *The Meaning of Truth*, p. 142.

71. *Ibid.*, pp. v-vi.

72. William James, *Essays in Radical Empiricism*, p. 94.

73. *Ibid.*, p. 93.

74. William James, II, p. 545; Edward C. Moore, *American Pragmatism: Peirce, James, and Dewey* (New York: Columbia University Press, 1961), p. 156.

75. William James, *Pragmatism* (New York: World Publishing Co., 1967), p. 135.

76. *Ibid.*, pp. 133, 136-137.

77. The *Hui-cheng-lun*, 24-26 and 57.

78. *Ibid.*, 30-50.

79. Seng-chao, *Chao-lun*, Part III in T. 1858, pp. 153a, 153c.

Chapter Five

Nāgārjuna, Kant and Wittgenstein

1. T.R.V. Murti, *The Central Philosophy of Buddhism* (London: George Allen and Unwin, 1970), p. 297.

2. Frederick J. Streng, *Emptiness: A Study in Religious Meaning* (New York: Abingdon Press, 1967), p. 139.

3. Ives Waldo, "Nāgārjuna and Analytic Philosophy, II," *Philosophy East and West*, XXVIII, 3 (July, 1978), p. 288. Chris Gudmunsen also states, "Nāgārjuna and Wittgenstein, by contrast, stand out as defending the 'mundane and customary' uses of words." *Wittgenstein and Buddhism* (New York: Barnes and Noble, 1977), p. 87.

4. Chris Gudmunsen, *Ibid.*, p. 115.

5. Immanuel Kant, *Critique of Pure Reason*, translated by Norman Kemp Smith (New York: St. Martin's Press, 1965), B 312, p. 273.

6. *Ibid.*

7. *Ibid.*, B 311, p. 272.

8. *Ibid.*, B 307, p. 268.

9. Immanuel Kant, *Prolegomena to Any Future Metaphysics*, translated by J.P. Mahaffy and J.H. Bernard (London, 1889), 13, remark 2.

10. See Kant, *Critique of Pure Reason*, B 391-392, pp. 323-324.

11. Kant, *Ibid.*, B 147, p. 162.

12. *Ibid.*, B 294, p. 256.

13. *Ibid.*, B 33, p. 65.

14. See the *Twelve Gate Treatise*, I. See also the *Middle Treatise*, I: 2, 13 and 15.

15. The *Middle Treatise*, III: 3 and 4.

16. T.R.V. Murti, *op. cit.*, p. 294.

17. Kant, *op. cit.*, B 350, p. 297.

18. The *Middle Treatise*, XIII: 8. Nāgārjuna also said: "Nothing could be asserted to be *śūnya* (empty), *aśūnya* (non-empty), both *śūnya* and *aśūnya*, and neither *śūnya* nor *aśūnya*. They are stated as provisionary names." *Ibid.*, XXII: 11.

19. Chi-tsang, *A Commentary on the Middle Treatise* (T1824), pp. 111-113; *The Profound Meaning of Three Treatises*, pp. 5-6 and 10-11; *The Meaning of Twofold Truth*, pp. 82, 87a, 91a, 94, 108c and 114b.

20. Kant said, "The transcendental illusion (metaphysical

speculation)...does not cease even after it has been detected and its invalidity clearly revealed by transcendental criticism." *Op. cit.*, B 353, p. 299.

21. In India philosophical study of the nature of words and its relation to meaning occurred in the *Jaimini-sūtra*, the *Nyāya-sūtra* and the *Vaiśeṣika-sūtra* from 500 B.C. to 200 A.D.

22. See Dhirendra Sharma, *The Differentiation Theory of Meaning in Indian Logic* (Hague: Mouton, 1969), p. 23, and S. Radhakrishnan and C.A. Moore, ed., *A Source Book in Indian Philosophy* (Princeton University Press, 1957), pp. 356, 386, 425 and 487. See also R.C. Pandeya, *The Problem of Meaning in Indian Philosophy* (Delhi: Motilal Banarsidass, 1963), pp. 188 and 206.

23. Generally speaking, the Mimāṁsā School is representative of the latter view and maintains that a word refers to a genus and only indirectly to a particular. The Nyāya School is a representative of the former view and holds that a word refers to an individual, the class residing in the individual and its configuration or form.

24. The *Middle Treatise*, XXV: 24.

25. *Ibid.*, XXII: 1b.

26. The *Hui-cheng-lun*, 22, 23, 55 and 57.

27. *Ibid.*, 25.

28. Seng-chao, *Chao-lun*, p. 152c.

29. Seng-jui, "Preface" in the *Twelve Gate Treatise*, p. 159b.

30. The *Middle Treatise*, XXVII: 30.

31. Chris Gudmunsen, *op. cit.*, pp. 68-69.

32. Ludwig Wittgenstein, *Philosophical Investigations*, translated by G.E.M. Anscombe (New York: Macmillan Co., 1968), pp. 20 and 128.

33. K.T. Fann, *Wittgenstein's Conception of Philosophy* (Berkeley: University of California Press, 1969), p. 68.

34. Wittgenstein, *op. cit.*, p. 45.

35. *Ibid.*, pp. 51-52.

36. *Ibid.*, p. 48.

37. *Ibid.*, p. 47.

38. *Ibid.*, p. 49. Wittgenstein also said, "We must do away with all *explanation*, and description alone must take its place." *Ibid.*, p. 47.

39. According to Henry Le Roy Finch, Wittgenstein's dualistic way of thinking is essentially Kantian: "Kant's innovation, the presuppositional method, dividing the world into the *a priori* and the *a posteriori*, is capable, we now see, of replacing the Cartesian division of *inner* and *outer* entirely. This is what Wittgenstein's philosophy showed, for it carried the Kantian method to the point of *wiping out the inner world of private objects altogether*.... Wittgenstein, who put *all* meaning into the presuppositional (even when, as in the later philosophy, this was regarded as only an aspect of the phenomenal), is the *ultimate Kantian*...." *Wittgenstein—The Later Philosophy: An Exposition of the*

Philosophical Investigations (Atlantic Highlands, N.J.: Humanities Press, 1977), p. 248.

40. See Wittgenstein, *On Certainty*, eds. G.E.M. Anscombe and G.H. von Wright, trans. D. Paul and G.E.M. Anscombe (Oxford: Blackwell, 1969), pp. 115, 219, 341, 354, 450, 519 and 625.

41. Wittgenstein described ordinary certainty as "the foundation of all judging" (*Ibid.*, pp. 308 and 614), "the foundation of all operating with thoughts" (*Ibid.*, p. 401), "the substratum of all my inquiring and asserting" (*Ibid.*, pp. 88, 151 and 162).

42. The *Twelve Gate Treatise*, VI: 1.

43. *Ibid.*, V: 1. See also the *Middle Treatise*, V: 1-5.

44. Wittgenstein stated that "It is only in normal cases that the use of the word is clearly prescribed; we know, are in no doubt, what to say in this or that case." *Philosophical Investigations*, p. 56.

45. The *Middle Treatise*, XVIII: 5b.

46. Chi-tsang, *The Meaning of the Twofold Truth*, p. 94c.

47. Seng-chao, *op. cit.*, p. 153c.

LIST OF CHINESE TERMS

Ch'an	禪
ch'ang	常
Ch'ang-an	長安
Chao-lun	肇論
chen-k'ung wu-hsiang	真空無相
chen-su erh-t'i	真俗二諦
chen-t'i	真諦
Chen-yen Tsung	真言宗
cheng-chien	正見
Cheng-shih Tsung	成實宗
Chi-tsang	吉藏
chi-yen chi-hsing	奇言奇行
chia-hsiang	假相

Chia-hsiang Ta-shih	嘉祥大師
chia-ming	假名
ch'iang-ming-cheng	強名正
chiao-t'i	教諦
chih	知
chin-sheng	今生
ching	經
Ching-t'u Tsung	淨土宗
ch'ü-shih	去時
ch'üan	諸說中第一
chu-shuo chung ti-i	荃
Chuang-tzu	莊子
Chung-kuan lun-su	中觀論疏
Chung-lun	中論
chung-tao	中道
erh-t'i-i	二諦義
erh-t'i-san-kuan	二諦三觀
fa	法

Fa-hsiang Tsung	法相宗
Fa-lang	法朗
Fa-tsang	法藏
fang-pien	方便
fei-yu fei-wu	非有非無
hsi-lun	戲論
hsiang	相
hsing	性
hsing-hsiang	性相
hsü	虛
Hsuan Tsang	玄奘
Hua-yen Tsung	華嚴宗
Hui-cheng-lun	迴諍論
Hui-neng	慧能
Hui-yuan	慧遠
i	義
I Ching	易經
i-ch'u	·己去

i-sheng 己生

jen-sheng hsi-lun 人生戲論

k'o-hsiang 可相

k'o-p'o 可破

k'ung 空

lao 老

Lao-tzu 老子

Liu I-min 劉遺民

Liu-tsu t'an-ching 六祖壇經

lun 論

Lung-shu 龍樹

Lung-shu-p'u-sa-chuan 龍樹菩薩傳

ming 名

nien-p'an 涅槃

nien-p'an-wu-ming 涅槃無名

pa-pu-chung-tao 八不中道

Pai-lun 百論

pan-jo-wu-chih 般若無知

p'o-hsieh-hsien-cheng 破邪顯正

pu-chen-k'ung 不真空

San-lun-hsüan-i 三論玄義

San-lun Tsung 三論宗

san-tsung-erh-t'i 三種二諦

Seng-chao 僧肇

Seng-ch'uan 僧詮

Seng-jui 僧叡

Seng-lang 僧朗

shan-mieh chu hsi-lun 善滅諸戲論

shen 神

shen-wo 神我

sheng 生

sheng-sheng 生時

sheng-shr 生生

shih 事

shih 實

shih 識

Shih-erh-men-lun	十二門論
Shih-erh-men-lun-chung-chih-i-chi	十二門論宗致義記
shih-hsiang	實相
su-t'i	俗諦
Ta-ch'eng ta-i-chang	大乘大義章
Ta-chih-tu-lun	大智度論
T'ai-hsü	太虛
Tao-te-ching	道德經
t'i	體
T'i-p'o	提婆
T'i-p'o-p'u-sa-chuan	提婆菩薩傳
t'ien	天
T'ien-t'ai Tsung	天台宗
ting-hsing	定性
tseng-shang-yüan	增上緣
tzu-hsing	自性
Tzu-tsai-t'ien	自在天
tz'u-ti-yüan	次第緣

wei-ch'ü   未去

wei-sheng   未生

wo   我

wu   無

wu   悟

wu   物

wu-lou   無漏

wu-hsin   無心

wu-pu-ch'ien   物不遷

wu-wei   無為

wu-wu   無物

wu-yin   五陰

wu-yin   無因

yin-yüan   因緣

yu   有

yu-lou   有漏

yu-wei-fa   有為法

yu-wu   有無

yüan 緣

yüan-yüan 緣緣

yung 用

GLOSSARY

Note: P = Pāli. S = Sanskrit. Ch = Chinese. Jap = Japanese.

Abhidhamma (P), Abhidharma (S): "Higher doctrine," "super-doctrine," dealing with Buddhist philosophy and psychology, the third division of the Pāli canon of scripture.

Āgama (P & S): General name for Hīnayāna or Theravāda scriptures, *Sutta Piṭaka* (P). There are five sections.
1. *Dīgha-nikāya* (P), *Dīrghāgama* (S). Long discourse.
2. *Majjhima-nikāya* (P), *Madhyamāgama* (S). Medium length discourse.
3. *Smyutta-nikāya* (P), *Samyuktāgama* (S). "Grouped" or "connected" discourse.
4. *Anguttara-nikāya* (P), *Ekottarāgama* (S). Numerical discourse.
5. *Khuddaka-nikāya* (P), *Ksuddakāgama* (S). Division of smaller books.

Ālaya-viññāna (P), Ālaya-vijñāna (S): The store-consciousness or the eighth consciousness in the Yogācāra school. It is the store-house or the basis from which all seeds of consciousness are stored.

Amitābha (S), Amitāyus (S), Omito (Ch), Amida (Jap): The Buddha of Infinite Light and Boundless Age. The founder of

167

Sukhāvatī, the Western Paradise. The object of worship in the Pure Land school.

Anattā (P), Anātman (S): Non-ego or non-self; the denial of the *Ātman* (of Hindu philosophy) conceived as a personal immortal soul or a substantial self.

Anicca (P), Anitya (S): Impermanence, change.

Anuttara-sammā-sambodhi (P), Anuttara-samyak-sambodhi (S): Unexcelled complete enlightenment; an attribute of every *buddha*.

Arahant (P), Arhat (S): The worthy one; a saintly man, the highest type or ideal in Hīnayāna, comparable to a *bodhisattva*, the saint in Mahāyāna.

Asaṃskhata (P), Asaṃskṛta (S): Unconditioned or non-created things.

Attā (P), Ātman (S): Ego, self, soul, or individual personality. In Brāhmanism, the Absolute, the unconditioned, the spirit, *Brahman*: also the reflection of the Absolute in the individual.

Avijja (P), Avidyā (S): Ignorance; lack of enlightenment.

Āyatana (P & S): Sense-fields. There are twelve, corresponding to the six sense faculties (five senses and the mind) and their objects.

Bhāvaviveka (Bhavya or Bhāviveka): The founder of the Svātantrika school of the Mādhyamika. He criticized Prāsangika Mādhyamika for merely indulging in refutation without advancing a counter-position and claimed that the true Mādhyamika could consistently advance an opposite view.

Bhikkhu (P), Bhikshu (S): A member of the Buddhist *Saṅgha* (Monastic Order). Often translated as monks or brethren.

Bhūmi (S): "Earth," or a stage. There are ten successive enlightenment stages of a *bodhisattva.*

Bhūmiśvara (S): One who has mastered the ten *bodhisattva* stages and arrived at unconditioned, absolute existence.

Bodhi (P & S): Enlightenment, enlightened mind, perfect wisdom, illumination, intuition, or inner light.

Bodhicitta (P & S): Heart-of-wisdom, thought-of-enlightenment, the divine spark of the Buddha-nature in the heart.

Bodhisatta (P), Bodhisattva (S): Wisdom-being. It was first used in the sense of a previous incarnation of the Buddha. Many lives before his final birth as Siddhartha Gautama the Bodhisattva did mighty deeds of compassion and self-sacrifice, as he gradually perfected himself in wisdom and virtue. In Mahāyāna, the *bodhisattva* is the ideal of the Path comparable to the *arhat* of the Theravāda. He is any individual self-dedicated to the salvation of others and destined to the attainment of Buddhahood.

Brahman (S): The Absolute, the Ultimate Substratum of all things.

Buddha (P & S): The Awakened or Enlightened One. (1) Siddhartha Gautama, after attaining enlightenment; (2) other individuals who have similarly attained enlightenment.

Buddhaghosa: A great Buddhist scholar, commentator and writer. Born in India, he moved to Ceylon about A.D. 430.

Almost all the commentaries now existing in Pāli are ascribed to him.

Buddhi (P & S): Enlightenment, intelligence, intuition, the faculty of direct awareness of Reality.

Candrakīrt: An important philosopher of Prāsangika Mādhyamika Buddhism of the seventh century. It was due to his efforts that *prasanga* (*reductio ad absurdum*) became the real and only method of Mādhyamika reasoning.

Ch'an (Ch): The Chinese word for *dhyāna*, or meditation. The Ch'an school was founded by Bodhidarma, and is known as Zen Buddhism to the West.

Chen-yen Tsung (Ch): The True Word School. "True Word" is a translation of the Sanskrit term *mantra*, which means a mystic doctrine that cannot be expressed in ordinary words. This school aims at the Buddha's own ideal not expressed in any way. It was introduced to Japan by Kōbō Daishi (Kūkai) from China in the ninth century, and is called the Shingon school in Japan.

Cheng-shih Tsung (Ch): The Chinese Satyasiddhi School. It asserts that nothing exists at all, and is called Jōjitsu in Japanese.

Chi-tsang (Ch): The greatest Chinese San-lun philosopher of the seventh century. He worked in the Chia-hsiang monastery and was known as Chia-hsiang Ta-shih (the Great Master Chia-hsiang).

Ching (Ch): Scripture.

Ching-t'u Tsung (Ch): The Pure Land School. *Ching-t'u* is a translation of the Sanskrit term *Sukhavati* (Land of Bliss). It is called Jōdo in Japanese. According to this school, anyone who believes in Amita Buddha will be born in the Pure Land to become a Buddha.

Chung-lun (Ch): The *Middle Treatise* (T 1564 in vol. 30). One of three main texts of the San-lun school. It was translated by Kumārajīva in 409 A.D. from the now lost *Mādhyamika-śāstra*. The main verses were written by Nāgārjuna, and its commentary was given by Piṅgala.

Daśabhūmi (S): The ten highest stages of *bodhisattva* attainment.

Deva (P & S): A god, angel, or benevolent celestial being.

Dhamma (P), Dharma (S): Truth, law, norm, doctrine, teaching, sermon, righteousness, morality, religion or doctrine; a thing, fact, element, factor, mark, attribute or quality.

Dhammakāya (P), Dharmakāya (S): The Body of Law. The Buddha as the personification of the Truth. The first of the threefold body of a Buddha.

Dhammapada (P): The Path or the Way of the Buddha's *Dharma* or Teaching. The most famous Scripture in the Pāli Canon. A collection of 423 verses comprising a noble system of moral philosophy.

Dhātus (S): Element, factor, or constituent.

Dhyāna (S): Meditation, or direct absorption in truth.

Dīgha-nikāya (P), Dīrghāgama (S): The collection of Long Discourses in the First Section of the *Sutta Piṭaka* (P).

Dukkha (P), Duhkha (S): Suffering, sorrow, or pain.

Dvādasa-dvāra-Śāstra (S): The *Twelve Gate Treatise*. One of three main texts of San-lun Buddhism.

Eightfold Noble Path: Right view, right thought, right speech, right action, right livelihood, right effort, right mindfulness and right concentration.

Fa (Ch), Dhamma (P), Dharma (S): A thing, fact, element, mark, truth, law, doctrine, norm, teaching, sermon, morality.

Fa-hsiang Tsung (Ch): Chinese Yogācāra School.

Five skandhas (S): Five aggregates. The sole constituents of personality. They are form (*rūpa*), feelings (*vedanā*), perceptions (*Sañjñā*), impulses (*samskāra*) and consciousness (*vijñāna*).

Four clingings: The clingings of passions, dogmatic views, rigid rules of conduct and selfhood.

Four Noble Truths: Catu Ariya Sacca (P), Catvāri Ārya Satyāna (S). The four basic principles of Buddhism preached by Buddha in his first sermon:
1. *Dukkha* (P), *Duhkha* (S). Suffering or sorrow.
2. *Samudaya* (P & S). The cause of suffering.
3. *Nirodha* (P & S). The cessation of suffering.
4. *Magga* (P), *Mārga* (S). The way leading to the cessation of suffering.

Four subsidiary causes: (1) The cause or chief condition (*Hetu-pratyaya*) which acts as the chief cause; for example, the wind and water that cause the wave. (2) The immediate condition (*Samanantara-pratyaya*) which immediately follows a preceding condition, such as waves following each other. (3) The objective condition (*Ālambana-pratyaya*). It is the objective (or subjective) environment, as concurring cause; for example, waves are conditioned by the basin or the boat or the pond. And (4) the upheaving condition (*Adhipati-pratyaya*), that which brings all conditions to the climax, such as the last wave that upsets the boat.

Gotama (P), Gautama (S): The clan name of the Buddha's family.

Hīnayāna (P): The Small Vehicle (of achieving *nirvāṇa*), a derogatory appellation given by the Mahāyānists to denote early Buddhist schools, of which the Theravāda is the sole survivor.

Hsu-lun (Ch): The Indian Sāmkya.

Hsuan-tsang (Ch): An important Chinese Buddhist translator and commentator of the seventh century.

Hua-yen Tsung (Ch): Chinese Avataṁsaka school. It is known as the Kegon school in Japan.

Hundred Treatise: The *Pai-lun* (Ch): T 1569 in vol. 30. It was translated by Kumārajīva in 404 A.D. from the *Śata-śāstra*. Its main verses were given by Āryadeva and its commentary was given by Vasu.

Īsvara (S): Overlord, a Supreme Personal God.

Jātaka (P & S): A birth-story, the history of some episode in the former lives of the Buddha. This is a book of the *Khuddaka-nikāya* (P).

Jih-chao (Ch): An Indian Buddhist who brought Sautrāntika-Svātantrika-Mādhyamika Buddhism to China from India in the seventh century. His Indian name is Divākara.

Kalpa (S): An eon, world period, or long space of time.

Kamma (P), Karma (S): Action, work, deed or product; the mysterious power which causes all action to work itself out in requital in another life; moral action which causes future retribution, and either good or evil transmigration.

Kumārajīva: A great Buddhist scholar of the fifth century. He introduced Mādhyamika Buddhism to China, and is noted for the number of his translations and commentaries.

K'ung (Ch): Emptiness or voidness.

Mādhyamika (S): The Middle-Way school founded by Nāgārjuna. It is known as San-lun Buddhism in China.

Mādhyamika-Kārika: The *Middle-Way Stanzas*, the original text of Mādhyamika teaching written by Nāgārjuna.

Magga (P), Mārga (S): Path or way. It is generally used to describe the Eightfold Noble Path or the Middle Way.

Mahāyāna (P & S): The Great Vehicle (of achieving *nirvāṇa*). Sometimes called the Northern School, of China, Korea, Japan, Tibet and Mongolia.

Mano-vijñāna (S): Thought center.

Middle Treatise: The *Chung-lun* (Ch): T 1564 in vol. 30. This treatise was translated by Kumārajīva in 409 A.D. from the now lost *Mādhyamika-śāstra*. The main verses were written by Nāgārjuna, and its commentary was given by Piṅgala.

Ming (Ch): Name, or symbol.

Nāga (P & S): Dragon, elephant or serpent.

Nāgārjuna: The great Buddhist philosopher of the second century. He taught distinctively the Mahāyāna doctrine of emptiness and founded Mādhyamika Buddhism. According to tradition, he discovered many Mahāyāna texts and established the Mahāyāna School of Buddhism, and hence was often called the "father of Mahāyāna."

Nibbāna (P), Nirvāṇa (S): Lit. "Extinction," or to be extinguished; to cease blowing; to be liberated from existence; freedom from desire. The supreme goal of Buddhist endeavor; release from the limitations of existence. The word is derived from a root meaning "extinguished through lack of fuel." *Nirvāṇa* is a state attainable in this life by right aspiration of life, and the elimination of egoism. One who has attained to this state is called an *arhant* and, at the death of his physical body, he attains complete *nirvāṇa* in which all attributes relating to phenomenal existence cease. In the Buddhist scriptures, the Buddha speaks of it as "an unborn, unoriginated, uncreated, unformed," contrasting it with the born, originated, created and formed phenomenal world. The Hīnayāna tends to view *nirvāṇa* as escape from life by overcoming its attraction, but the Mahāyāna views it as the fruition of life, the unfolding of the infinite possibilities of the innate buddha-nature, and exalts the saint who remains in touch with life, rather than the saint who relinquishes all connection with it.

Nikāya (P & S): A chapter or section of the Discourse, *Sutta* (P) or *Sūtra* (S).

Nirodha (P & S): Cessation, extinction, or extermination. It often refers to the third noble truth, the cessation of suffering.

Pai-lun (Ch): See the *Hundred Treatise.*

Pāli (P): One of the early languages of Buddhism. It was later adopted by the Thervādins as the language in which to preserve the memorized teachings of the Buddha.

Pāli Canon: The Three Baskets of the Scripture, i.e. *Suttapiṭaka*, *Vinayapiṭaka* and *Abhidhammapiṭaka*, in the Pāli language. The Canon contains the main sacred texts of Theravāda Buddhism. It was compiled and edited by three monastic councils. The First Council assembled just a few months after the death of the Buddha (483 B.C.) in Rājagaha, the Second about a hundred years later (around 383 B.C.) in Vesāli, the Third in 225 B.C. in Pātaliputta.

Pan-jo Tsung (Ch): Chinese Wisdom School.

Paññā (P), Prajñā (S): Wisdom, reason, insight.

Paramārtha satya (S): Ultimate or absolute truth.

Pāramitā (P & S): Transcendental perfection, especially the perfected virtue of a *bodhisattva*. In Mahāyāna Buddhism, there are usually six major *pāramitās*: charity, discipline, vigor, patience, meditation and intuitive wisdom.

Paratantra (S): The dependent or caused character of things. This is the Yogācārin version of dependent-arising, that all things are manifestations of mind, and mind is a group of consciousness mutually dependent for their continuous existence and function.

Parikalpita (S): The illusory or imaged character of things; the erroneous idea of considering the phenomenal world to be truly existent and outside of one's mind; the great delusion.

Parinibbāna (P), Parinirvāna (S): The final or complete *Nirvāna*, the *Nirvāna* attained at the moment of death which forever relinquishes the burdens of *samsāric skandhas*.

Parinshpana (S): The absolute reality or ultimate knowledge.

Paticcasamuppāda (P), Pratītyasamutpāda (S): Dependent origination or arising, causality.

Pitaka (P): Lit. "basket." The Buddhist Pāli Canon is called the Pitakas, or the *Tipitaka* (three baskets).

Prajñāpāramitā (S): The perfection of wisdom, the paramount practice and virtue of a *bodhisattva*; the last of six *pāramitās* consisting in the perfect arousal and exercise of inner wisdom for the purpose of crossing over from this shore of mortality, or *samsāra*, to the other shore, or *Nirvāna*.

Prāsangika: One of two major Mādhyamika schools. It was founded by Buddhapālita (*c.* 400-450 A.D.). According to this school, the real and true method of Nāgārjuna and Āryadeva is *prasanga* (*reductio ad absurdum*). The true Mādhyamika does not and should not uphold any position of his own.

Pratyeka Buddhas (S): "Private" or "lonely" *buddhas*, so called because they reap the fruits of their striving without returning to share that merit with mankind.

Rāhula: The name of Prince Siddhartha's (Buddha's) only son.

Rūpa (P & S): Form, matter, body. The first aggregate.

Sākya (P & S): The clan to which Gotama the Buddha belonged.

Śākyamuni (P & S): The sage or holy man of the Sākyas. A title given to the Buddha by those outside the Sākya clan.

Samādhi (P & S): Meditation, contemplation, concentration, rapture, tranquility.

Sāmkhya (S): "School of the Count," a pre-Buddhist philosophy, so-called as "reckoning-up" the twenty-five categories.

Samsāra (P & S): Lit. "faring on" or "coming-to-be"; the world of becoming; the realm of birth and death. *Samsāra* is symbolically referred to as "this shore," *Nirvāna* as "the other shore," and *Dharma* as "the raft" which carries us across.

Samskhata (P), Samskrta (S): Conditioned or created things and states.

Samudaya (P & S): Cause of suffering; the second noble truth.

Samuvrti-satya (S): Conventional, relative or worldly truth.

San-lun Tsung (Ch): Lit. "Three Treatise School." Chinese Mādhyamika Buddhism.

San-lun-hsüan-i (Ch): The title of the book *The Profound Meaning of Three Treatises* (T 1852 in vol. 45), written by Chi-tsang.

Sangha (P & S): The Order, the assembly or congregation of

monks and nuns; the third of three jewels of Buddha, *Dharma* and *Saṅgha*.

Sanskrit: The classical Aryan language of India. Most of the Mahāyāna texts were written in Sanskrit.

Śata-śāstra (S): See the *Hundred Treatise*.

Satthā (P), Śāstra (S): To discuss; discussion; treatises on dogma, philosophy, discipline, science or art.

Sautrāntikas: Buddhists who hold the *Sūtras* as their authority and not the *Śāstras*. They do not admit the authority of the *Abhidharma* of the Sarvastivadins. They assert the reality of both physical objects and the mind, but claim that we do not have a direct perception of external objects.

Seng-chao: An important Chinese San-lun philosopher of the fifth century. The author of the *Chao-lun*.

Seng-jui: An important Chinese San-lun philosopher of the fifth century. He wrote prefaces to the *Middle Treatise* and the *Twelve Gate Treatise*.

Sheng (Ch): Production, origination.

Shih-erh-men-lun (Ch): The *Twelve Gate Treatise* (T 1568 in vol. 30). One of three main texts of San-lun Buddhism. It was translated by Kumārajīva in 408-409 A.D. from the now lost *Dvādasa-dvāra-Śāstra*. Both main verses and commentary were given by Nāgārjuna.

Siddhattha Gotama (P), Siddhārta Gautama (S): The name of the Buddha, the founder of Buddhism. It was given by his father, King Suddhodana of Kapilavatthu.

Sīla (P & S): Precept, virtue, morality, discipline, rule.

Six famous Tīrthikas: A Tīrthika is an heretical or non-Buddhist religious man. Six famous Tīrthikas or heretical teachers were Pūraṇa-Kāśyapa, Maskarin, Sañjayin, Ajita-kesakambala, Kakuda-Kātyāyana and Nirgrantha.

Six forms of life: Hellish things, hungry spirits, beasts, evil spirits, human beings, and heavenly beings.

Six pāramitās (P & S): Six perfections. They are charity, moral conduct, patience, devotion, contemplation and knowledge.

Six sense organs: Eye, ear, nose, tongue, body and mind.

Skandhas (S): Aggregates or heaps. The five *skandhas* are the sole constituents of the personality. The so-called "I" or "ego" is but a collection of aggregates of various elements, and hence there is no eternal self within.

Śramana (S): An ascetic.

Śrāvaka (S): A hearer, disciple of the Buddha who understands the Four Noble Truths, rids himself of the unreality of the phenomenal and enters the incomplete *nirvāṇa*. It is used by Mahāyānists, in conjunction with *Pratyeka Buddha*, to describe those of the Old Wisdom Schools.

Ssu-lun Chung (Ch): The Four Treatises School.

Śūnya (S): Empty, void, vacant, non-existent.

Śūnyatā (S): Emptiness, voidness, non-existence.

Sutta (P), Sūtra (S): Lit. a thread or string on which jewels are strung; a sermon or discourse of the Buddha. It often refers to that part of the Pāli Canon containing the narratives about dialogues by the Buddha. A number of Mahāyāna scriptures are also called *sūtras*.

Svabhāva (S): "Own-nature"; self-existence, self-being, self-hood, that which does not depend on others for its existence.

Svātantrika: One of the two major schools of Mādhyamika Buddhism. It was founded by Bhāvaviveka in the sixth century. According to this school, empirical things are not real from the standpoint of ultimate truth, yet have phenomenal reality. Svātantrika Mādhyamikas criticized Prāsangika Mādhyamikas for merely indulging in refutation without advancing a counter-position and claimed that the true Mādhyamika could consistently advance an opposite view.

Ta-chih-tu-lun (Ch): The *Great Wisdom Treatise* (T 1852 in vol. 45).

Tariki (Jap): Salvation by some "other power."

Tathāgata (P & S): Thus-gone or Thus-come, He-who-has-thus-attained, a title of the Buddha used by his followers and also by himself.

Tathatā (P & S): Suchness; thusness, i.e. such is its nature; the absolute reality beyond all designations. The only appropriate description is to call it "suchness."

Theravāda (P), Sthaviravāda (S): "The system or school of the Elders," considered to be the orthodox and original form of Buddhism as accepted and followed mainly in Ceylon, Burma, Thailand, Laos and Cambodia.

Three Jewels: Tiratana (P), Triratna (S). Three Jewels of Buddhism are Buddha, *Dharma* and *Saṅgha*. For monks and laymen initiation into Buddhism starts with a proclamation of allegiance, which runs like this:
> "I take my refuge in the Buddha.
> I take my refuge in the *Dharma*.
> I take my refuge in the *Saṅgha*."

T'i-p'o-p'u-sa-ch'uan (Ch): The *Biography of Bodhisattva Āryadeva* (T 2048).

T'ien-t'ai Tsung (Ch): The Chinese Buddhist school founded by Chih-i (Chih-kai, 531-597 A.D.). It was also called the Fa-hua after the title of the text *Saddharma-puṇḍarika* from which the doctrine of the school is derived.

Tikāya (P), Trikāya (S): The Mahāyāna doctrine of the threefold body or nature of a Buddha:
1. *Dharmakāya* (S), the absolute or spiritual body.
2. *Sambhagakāya* (S), the body of bliss.
3. *Nirmāṇakāya* (S), the body of incarnation.

Tipiṭaka (P), Tripiṭaka (S): The Three Baskets:
1. *Sutta* (P), *Sūtra* (S). Doctrine, discourse.
2. *Vinaya* (P & S). Rules of discipline.
3. *Abhidhamma* (P), *Abhidharma* (S). Discussion, metaphysics.

Tīrthika: A heretic in India.

Twelve āyatanas (P & S): Twelve sense fields; eye, sight-objects, ear, sounds, nose, smells, tongue, tastes, body, touchable, mind and mind-objects.

Twelve Gate Treatise: See *Shih-erh-men-lun*.

Tzu-tai-t'ien (Ch): Ĭsvara (S): Overlord, a Supreme Personal God.

Upaniṣads (S): A class of philosophical treatises attached to the Brahmāna portion of the *Vedas*.

Upāya (P & S): Convenience, as convenient method or device.

Vasubandu: A great philosopher of the Mind-Only teaching in the fifth century. He and his brother, Asanga, founded the Yogācāra School.

Vinaya (P & S): Rules of the Buddhist Order; one of the three baskets of the Pāli Canon.

Viññāna (P), Vijñāna (S): Consciousness.

Wei-sheng (Ch): That which is not yet produced or originated.

Wei-shih (Ch): Vaiśeṣika.

Wu (Ch): Nothing, non-being, emptiness.

Wu (Ch): Thing.

Wu-hsin (Ch): No thought or mind.

Wu-wei (Ch): Nonaction, passivity, action without action.

Wu-yin (Ch): Five *skandhas*, five aggregates.

Yoga (P & S): "Yoke" in the sense of "that which unites," therefore "Union." The Hindu system of discipline, which brings a man to union with Reality.

Yogācāra (P & S): The Mind-Only School of Buddhism, founded by Asanga and Vasubandu.

Yu (Ch): Being, existence.

Zen (Jap): The Japanese pronunciation of the Chinese ideograph for *Ch'an*, which is derived from the Sanskrit *dhyāna*; the Chinese and Japanese Meditation School of Buddhism, established by Bodhidharma, the 28th Patriarch in India, who came to China around 520 A.D. as the First Patriarch in China.

Selected Bibliography

Alston, William P., *Philosophy of Language*. Englewood Cliffs, N.J.: Prentice-Hall, 1964.

Anchō, *Chūron shoki* (A Commentary on the *Middle Treatise*), T 2255.

Āryadeva, *Kuang-pai-lun-pen* (The Broad Hundred Treatise), T 1570.
——, *Pai-lun* (The Hundred Treatise), T 1569.
——, *Pai-tzu-lun* (The Hundred Word Treatise), T 1572.

Baird, Robert D., "The Symbol of Emptiness and the Emptiness of Symbols," *Humanitas*, 8 (May, 1972), pp. 221-242.

Bhattacharya, A.R., "*Brahman* of Śankara and *Śūnyatā* of Mādhyamikas," *Indian Historical Quarterly*, XXXII (1956), pp. 270-285.

Bhattacharya, Kamaleswar, "The Dialectical Method of Nāgārjuna," *Journal of Indian Philosophy*, 1 (November, 1971), pp. 217-261.

Blofeld, John, *The Zen Teaching of Huang Po*. New York: Grove Press, 1958.

Brough, John, "Some Indian Theories of Meaning," *Transactions of the Philological Society* (1953), pp. 161-176.

Buston, Rin-chen-grub-pa, *History of Buddhism* (E. Obermiller, trans.) Heidelberg: Harrassowitz, 1931.

Chan, Wing-tsit, *A Source Book in Chinese Philosophy*. Princeton: Princeton University Press, 1972.

Chang, Chung-yuan, *Original Teachings of Ch'an Buddhism*. New York: Vintage Books, 1971.

Chang, Garma C.C., *The Buddhist Teaching of Totality*. University Park: The Pennsylvania State University Press, 1974.
——, *The Practice of Zen*. New York: Harper & Row, 1970.

Chang, Man-tao (ed.), *San-lun-tien-chi-yen-chiu* (Studies in San-lun Documents). Taipei: Ta-cheng-wen-hua Publishing Company, 1979.
——, *San-lun-tsung-chih-fa-chan-chi-ch'i-ssu-hsian* (The Development of San-lun School and Its Thought). Taipei: Ta-cheng-wen-hua Publishing Company, 1978.
——, *Chung-kuan-ssu-hsian-lun-chi* (The Collection of Essays on San-lun Thoughts). Taipei: Ta-cheng-wen-hua Publishing Company, 1978.

Chatterjee, Heramba Nath, *Mūla-Mādhyamika-Kārikā of Nāgārjuna*. Calcutta: Sanskrit College, 1957 (Par I; Chapters I-V), 1962 (Par II; Chapters VI-VII).

Ch'en, Kenneth, *Buddhism in China*. Princeton: Princeton University Press, 1964.
——, "Transformations in Buddhism in Tibet," *Philosophy East and West*, VII (October, 1957; January, 1958).

Cheng, Hsueh-li, *Nāgārjuna's Twelve Gate Treatise*. Boston: D. Reidel Publishing Company, 1982.

——, "Nāgārjuna's Approach to the Problem of the Existence of God," *Religious Studies*, No. 12 (June, 1976), pp. 207-216.

——, "The Problem of God in Buddhism," *The Theosophist*, Vol. 98, No. 9 (June, 1977), pp. 98-108.

——, "Zen and San-lun Mādhyamika Thought: Exploring the Theoretical Foundation of Zen Teachings and Practices," *Religious Studies*, No. 15 (September, 1979), pp. 343-363.

——, "Nāgārjuna, Kant and Wittgenstein: The San-lun Mādhyamika Exposition of Emptiness," *Religious Studies*, No. 17 (March, 1981), pp. 67-85.

——, "Motion and Rest in the *Middle Treatise*," *Journal of Chinese Philosophy*, No. 7 (September, 1980), pp. 229-244.

——, "Truth and Logic in San-lun Mādhyamika Buddhism," *International Philosophical Quarterly*, No. 21 (September, 1981), pp. 260-276.

——, "Chi-tsang's Treatment of Metaphysical Issues," *Journal of Chinese Philosophy*, No. 8 (September, 1981), pp. 371-389.

——, "Zen, Wittgenstein and Neo-orthodox Theology: The Problem of Communicating Truth in Zen Buddhism," *Religious Studies*, No. 18 (December, 1982), pp. 133-149.

——, "Causality as Soteriology: An Analysis of the Central Philosophy of Buddhism," *Journal of Chinese Philosophy*, No. 9 (December, 1982), pp. 423-440.

Chi-tsang, *Chung-kuan-lun-su* (A Commentary on the *Middle Treatise*), T 1824.

——, *Erh-tí-i* (The Meaning of Twofold Truth), T 1854.

——, *Pai-lun-su* (A Commentary on the *Hundred Treatise*), T 1827.

——, *San-lun-hsüan-i* (The Profound Meaning of Three Treatises), T 1852.

——, *Shih-erh-men-lun-su* (A Commentary on the *Twelve Gate Treatise*), T 1825.

Conze, Edward, *Buddhist Scriptures.* Baltimore: Penguin Books, 1966.
——, *Buddhist Thought in India.* Ann Arbor: The University of Michigan Press, 1967.
——, "Meditations on Emptiness," *The Maha Bodhi,* (May, 1955), pp. 203-211.

Coomaraswamy, Ananda K., *Buddha and the Gospel of Buddhism.* New York, Harper & Row, 1964.
——, *Hinduism and Buddhism.* Westport, Connecticut: Greenwood, 1971.

de Bary, William Theodore (ed.), *The Buddhist Tradition in India, China and Japan.* New York: Modern Library, 1969.
——, *Sources of Indian Tradition.* 2 vols. New York: Columbia University Press, 1958.

De Jong, Jan W., *Cinq chapitres de la Prasannapadā.* Paris: Geuthner, 1949.
——, "Emptiness," *Journal of Indian Philosophy,* 2 (December, 1972), pp. 7-15.
——, "The Problem of the Absolute in the Mādhyamika School," *Ibid.,* pp. 1-6.

Dumoulin, Heinrich, *A History of Zen Buddhism.* New York: Pantheon Books, 1963.
——, *The Development of Chinese Zen* (Ruth Fuller Sasaki, trans.). New York: The First Zen Institute of America Inc., 1953.

Edgerton, Franklin, *Buddhist Hybrid Sanskrit Dictionary.*

New Haven: Yale University Press, 1953.

Fa-tsang, *Shih-erh-men-lun tsung-chih-i-chi* (Notations on the *Twelve Gate Treatise*), T 1826.

Fang, Li-t'en, "A Tentative Treatise on the Buddhist Philosophical Thought of Hui-yuan," *Chinese Studies in Philosophy*, 4 (Spring, 1973), pp. 36-74.

Fujimoto, Ryukyo, *An Outline of the Triple Sutra of Shin Buddhism*, Vol. 1. Kyoto: Honpa Hongwanji Press, 1955.

Fung, Yu-lan, *A History of Chinese Philosophy* (Derk Bodde, trans.). 2 vols. Princeton: Princeton University Press, 1953.
——, *A Short History of Chinese Philosophy* (Derk Bodde, ed.). New York: The Free Press, 1966.

Gard, Richard A., "On the Authenticity of the *Pai-lun* and *Shih-erh-men-lun*," *Indogaku Bukkyōgaku Kenkyū*, II, no. 2 (1954), pp. 751-742.
——, "On the Authenticity of the *Chung-lun*," *Ibid.*, III, no. 1 (1954), pp. 376-370.

Hatani, Ryōtai, "Dialectics of the Mādhyamika Philosophy," *Studies on Buddhism in Japan*, Vol. 1. Tokyo: 1939, pp. 53-71.
——, *Sanron kaidai to honyaku* (Translations and Critical Analysis of the Three Treatises of the Mādhyamika), in Kokuyaku Issaikyō Chūganbu, Vol. I. Tokyo: Daitoshuppan-sha, 1930.

Hiriyanna, M., *Outlines of Indian Philosophy*. London: George Allen and Unwin Ltd., 1932.

Huang, Ch'an-hua, *Chung-kuo fo-chiao-shih* (History of

Chinese Buddhism). Shanghai: Commercial Press, 1940.

Huang, Kung-wei, *Chung-kuo fo-chaio-ssu-hsiang-ch'uan-t'ung-shih* (History of Chinese Buddhist Thought and Tradition). Taipei: Siao-lin, 1972.

Hurvitz, Leon, "The First Systematizations of Buddhist Thought in China," *Journal of Chinese Philosophy*, 2 (September, 1975), pp. 361-388.

In-shun (Shih-in-shun), *Cheng-fo-chih-tao* (The Way to Become Buddha). Taipei: Hui-jih Chiang-t'ang, 1971.
——, *Chung-kuan-chin-lun* (The Contemporary Study of The Middle Way). Taipei: Hui-jih Chiang-t'ang, 1971.
——, *Chung-kuan-lun-song-chiang-chi* (An Exposition of the *Middle Treatise*). Taipei: Hui-jih Chiang-t'ang, 1963.
——, *Hsing-k'ung-hsüeh-t'an-yüan* (Exploring the Source of the Emptiness of Essence). Taipei: Hui-jih Chiang-t'ang, 1963.

Inada, Kenneth K., *Nāgārjuna: A Translation of His Mūlamadhyamaka-kārikā with an Introductory Essay*. Tokyo: Hokuseido, 1970.

Inazu, Kizō, "Ryūju no chū no tetsugaku" (The Philosophy of *Madhyamāpratipad* in Nāgārjuna), *Indogaku Bukkyōgaku Ronshū* (Collection of Essays in Indology and Buddhology honoring Prof. Shōson Miyamoto). Tokyo: Sanseidō, 1954, pp. 269-276.

Jayatilleke, K.N., *Early Buddhist Theory of Knowledge*. London: George Allen & Unwin Ltd., 1963.
——, *The Message of the Buddha* (Ninian Smart, ed.). New York: The Free Press, 1975.

Kaiken, *Chūgwan ronhon shaku* (A Commentary on the *Middle Treatise*), T 2256.

Kajiyama, Y., "Bhāvaviveka and the Prāsangika School," *The Nava-Nalanda-Mahavihara Research Publication*, ed. S. Mookerjee, Nalanda, I (1957), pp. 289-331.

Kalupahana, David J., *Buddhist Philosophy: A Historical Analysis*. Honolulu: The University of Hawaii Press, 1976.
——, *Causality: The Central Philosophy of Buddhism*. Honolulu: The University of Hawaii Press, 1975.

Kamata, Shigeo, "Kūgan no chūgokuteki heni" (Chinese Modification of *Śūnyatā-vāda*), *Indogaku Bukkyōgaku Kenkyū*, XVI, No. 2 (1968), pp. 522-527.

Karambelkar, V.W., "The Problem of Nāgārjuna," *Journal of Indian History*, XXX, No. 1 (1952), pp. 21-33.

Keith, Arthur Berridale, *Buddhist Philosophy in India and Ceylon*. Oxford: The Clarendon Press, 1923.
——, *Indian Logic and Atomism*. London: Oxford University Press, 1921.

King, W.L., "*Śūnyatā* as a Master-symbol," *Numen, International Review for the History of Religions*, 17 (August, 1970), pp. 95-104.

Kitabatake, Toshichika, "Shōben to gesshō no nitairon" (The Twofold Truth of Bhāvaviveka and Candrakīrti), *Indogaku Bukkyōgaku Kenkyū*, XI, No. 1 (1963), pp. 66-71.

Kouan, Lin Li, "Á propos de la Sunyata (La Vide)," *La Pensée bouddhique*, No. 5 (Juillet, 1940), pp. 8-12.

Kudō, Shigeki, "Chūgan ni okeru jishō no gainen" (On the Concept of *Svabhāva* in the *Prasannapadā*), *Indogaku Bukkyōgaku Kenkyū*, VII, No. 1 (1958), pp. 174-175.

Kumārajīva, *Lung-shu-p'u-sa-chuan* (Biography of Bodhisattva Nāgārjuna), T 2047.
——, *T'i-p'o-p'u-sa-chuan* (Biography of Bodhisattva Āryadeva), T 2048.

Lamott, Étienne, *Le traité de la grande vertue de sagesse*, vol. 1, 1944; vol. II, 1949. Louvain: Bureaux du Muséon.
——, *"Mādhyamakavṛtti XVII Chaptre: Examen de l'acte et du fruit,"* *Mélanges chinois et bouddhiques*, IV. Bruxelles, 1936, pp. 265-288.

La Vallée Poussin, Louis de, *Mūlamadhyamakakārikās de Nāgārjuna avec la Prasannapadā de Candrakīrti* (*Bibliotheca Buddhica*, vol. IV). St. Petersburg: Imperial Academy of Sciences, 1913.
——, "Mādhyamika," *Encyclopedia of Religion and Ethics*, James Hastings (ed.), vol. VIII. Edinburgh: T. & T. Clark; New York: C. Scribner's Sons, 1916.
——, "Notes on *Śūnyatā* and the Middle Path," *Indian Historical Quarterly*, No. 4 (1928), pp. 161-168.
——, "The Mādhyamika and the Tathatā," *Ibid.*, IX (1933), pp. 30-31.

Law, B.C., "The Formulation of the *Pratītyasamutpāda*," *Journal of the Royal Asiatic Society*, 1937, pp. 287-292.

Lee, Shih-chieh, *San-lun-tsung-kang-yao* (The Essentials of the San-lun School). Taipei: Hsieh-lin, 1972.

Liebenthal, Walter, *The Book of Chao*. Peking: The Catholic University of Peking, 1948; Hong-Kong: Hong-Kong University, 1968.

May, Jacques, "La philosophie bouddhique de la vacuité," *Studia Philosophica*, XVIII (1958), pp. 123-137.

——, "Kant et le Mādhyamika," *Indo-Iranian Journal*, III (1959), pp. 102-111.

——, *Prasannapadā Madhyamakavṛtti, douze chapitres traduits du sanscrit et du tibétain*. Paris: Adrien-Maisonneuve, 1959.

McGovern, William M., *Manual of Buddhist Philosophy*. London: Kegan Paul, Trubner & Co., Ltd., 1923.

Mitsukawa, Toyoki, "Chūganha ni okeru shaki no ito surumono" (The Nature of Negation [*Pratiṣedha*] in the Mādhyamika School), *Indogaku Bukkyōgaku Kenkyū*, X, No. 1 (1962), pp. 255-260.

——, "Chūganha to buha tono kankei" (On the Relation between the Mādhyamika School and the Hīnayāna), *Ibid.*, VIII, No. 1 (1960), pp. 186-187.

Miyamoto, Shōson, *Chūdō shisō oyobi sono hattatsu* (Middle Way Thought and Its Development). Kyoto: Hōzōkan, 1944.

——, *Kompon chū to kū* (The Fundamental Middle and Emptiness). Tokyo: Daiichi Shobō, 1943.

——, "The Buddha's First Sermon and the Original Patterns of the Middle Way," *Indogaku Bukkyōgaku Kenkyū*, XIII, No. 2 (1965), pp. 855-845.

——, "The historico-social Bearings of the Middle Way," *Ibid.*, XIV, No. 2 (1966), pp. 996-969.

——, "Voidness and Middle Way," *Studies on Buddhism in Japan*, Volume one. Edited by the International Buddhist Society. Tokyo: 1939, pp. 73-92.

Mookerjee, Satkari, "The Absolutionists' Standpoint in Logic," in *The Nava-Nalanda-Mahavihara Research Publication*, Vol. I (1957), pp. 1-175.

Mukhopadhya, S., "Doctrine of Shunyata in Mahayana Buddhism," *Prabuddhi Bharata*, XLVIII (1943), pp. 327-329.

Murti, T.R.V., *The Central Philosophy of Buddhism*. London: Allen and Unwin, 1955.

Nagao, Gadjin M., "Chūgan tetsugaku no kompon teki tachiba" (The Fundamental Standpoint of the Mādhyamika Philosophy), *Tetsugaku Kenkyū*, Vol. 31 (1947), No. 9, pp. 1-27, No. 11, pp. 16-49. Vol. 32 (1948), No. 1, pp. 1-41, No. 2, pp. 19-38.
——, "The Silence of the Buddha and Its Mādhyamic Interpretation," *Indogaku Bukkyōgaku Ronsō* (Studies in Indology and Buddhology honoring Prof. Susumi Yamaguchi). Kyoto: Hozokan, 1955, pp. 137-151.

Nāgārjuna, *Chung-lun* (The Middle Treatise), T 1564.
——, *Hui-cheng-lun* (The Refutation Treatise), T 1631.
——, *Shih-erh-men-lun* (The Twelve Gate Treatise), T 1568.
——, *Ta-ch'eng-p'o-yu-lun* (Refutation of the Concept of Being in the Mahayana), T 1574.

Nakamura, Hajime, "Buddhist Logic Expounded by Means of Symbolic Logic," *Indogaku Bukkyōgaku Kenkyū*, VII, No. 1 (1958), pp. 395-375.

Narain, Harsh, "*Śūnyavāda*: A Reinterpretation," *Philosophy East and West*, XIII, No. 4 (January, 1964), pp. 311-338.

Nishida, Kitaro, *Intelligibility and the Philosophy of Nothingness* (Robert Schinzinger, trans.). Honolulu: East-West Center Press, 1958.

Nishitani, Keiji, *Religion and Nothingness* (Jan Van Bragt, trans.). University of California Press, 1982.

Obermiller, Evgenii E., "A Study of Twenty Aspects of *Śūnyatā* Based on Haribhadra's *Abhisamayālamkarāloka* and the *Pañcavimśatisahasrikā-prajñāpāramitā-sūtra*," *Indian Historical Quarterly*, IX (1933), pp. 170-187.
——, "The Term *Śūnyatā* and Its Different Interpretations," *Journal of the Greater Indian Society*, I (1934), pp. 105-117.

Pandeya, R.C., "The Mādhyamika Philosophy: A New Approach," *Philosophy East and West*, XIV, No. 1 (April, 1964), pp. 3-24.

Pannikar, R., "The Crisis of Mādhyamika and Indian Philosophy Today," *Ibid.*, XVI, Nos. 3 and 4 (July-October, 1966), pp. 117-131.

Patkok, Sunitkumar, "Life of Nāgārjuna," *Indian Historical Quarterly*, XXX (1954), pp. 93-95.

Potter, Karl H., *Presuppositions of India's Philosophies.* Englewood Cliffs, N.J.: Prentice-Hall, 1963.

Priestley, C.D.C., "Emptiness in the Satyasiddhi," *Journal of Indian Philosophy*, 1 (December, 1970), pp. 30-39.

Radhakrishnan, S., *Indian Philosophy.* 2 vols. London: George Allen and Unwin Ltd., 1966.
——, and Moore, C.A. (eds.), *A Source Book in Indian Philosophy.* Princeton: Princeton University Press, 1957.

Rahula, Walpola, *What The Buddha Taught.* New York: Grove Press, 1959.

Raju, P.T., "The Principle of Four-cornered Negation in Indian Philosophy," *Review of Metaphysics*, VII, No. 4 (June, 1954), pp. 694-713.

Ramanan, K. Venkata, "A Fresh Appraisal of the Mādhya-mika Philosophy," *Visvabharati Quarterly*, XXVII, No. 3/4 (1961/62), pp. 230-238.

——, *Nāgārjuna's Philosophy as Presented in the Mahapraj-ñāpāramitā Śāstra*. Varanasi, India: Bharatiya Vidya Praka-shan, 1971.

Randle, H.N., *Indian Logic in the Early Schools*. London: 1930.

Reischauer, August Karl, *Studies in Japanese Buddhism*. New York: 1925.

Robinson, Richard H., *Early Mādhyamika in India and China*. Madison: The University of Wisconsin Press, 1967.

——, "Mysticism and Logic in Seng-chao's Thought," *Philosophy East and West*, VIII, Nos. 3 and 4 (1958-59), pp. 99-120.

——, "Some Logical Aspects of Nāgārjuna's System," *Ibid.*, VI, No. 4 (January, 1957), pp. 291-308.

Saigusa, Mitsuyoshi, "Daichidoron ni tokareta roku hara-mitsu ni tsuite" (On the six *pāramitās* in the *Mahāprajñā-pāramitā-śāstra*), *Indogaku Bukkyōgaku Kenkyū*, II, No. 2 (1954), pp. 188-192.

——, "*Fa* and *Dharma* in Kumārajīva's *Mādhyamikakārikā*," *Ibid.*, XIII, No. 1 (1965), pp. 419-412.

——, "Ryūju no kū ti tsuite" (On the Concept of *śūnyatā* in Nāgārjuna), *Indogaku Bukkyōgaku Ronshū* (Collection of Essays in Indology and Buddhology honoring Prof. Shōson Miyamoto). Tokyo: Sanseidō, 1954, pp. 277-290.

——, "Ryūju no Hōben Shisō" (The Concept of Skillful Means in Nāgārjuna), *Indogaku Bukkyōgaku Kenkyū*, III, No. 1 (1954), pp. 232-235.

——, "Daichidron Shoshū geju to chūron ju" (Verses Quoted

in the *Mahāprajñāpāramitā-śāstra* and the *Mādhyamaka-kārikās*), *Ibid.*, XV, No. 1 (1966), pp. 85-97.

——, "Chūron ni okeru buddakan" (The Idea of Buddha in the *Middle Treatise*), *Ibid.*, XVI, No. 1 (1967), pp. 24-29.

——, *Chūron: Bon-kanzō Taishō goi* (An Index to the *Middle Treatise* in Sanskrit, Chinese and Tibetan). Tokyo: Sanseidō, 1959.

Sarkar, A.K., "Nāgārjuna: On Causation and *Nirvāṇa*," *Dr. S. Radhakrishnan Souvenir Volume*. Darshana, Moradabad, India, 1963, pp. 395-404.

Sastri, N.A., "Nāgārjuna and Satkaryavāda of the Śāṅkhyas," *Sino-Indian Studies*, IV (1950), pp. 47-50.

——, "Nāgārjuna on the Buddhist Theory of Causation," *Prof. K.V. Rangaswami Aiyangar Commemoration Volume*. Madras, 1940, pp. 485-492.

Sastri, P.S., "Nāgārjuna and Āryadeva," *Indian Historical Quarterly*, XXXI (1955), pp. 193-202.

Scaligero, Massimo, "The Doctrine of the Void and the Logic of the Essence," *East and West*, XI (1960), pp. 249-257.

Schayer, Stanislaw, *Ausgewählte Kapitel aus der Prasannapadā*. Krakow: Naktadem Polskiej Akademji Umiejetności, 1931.

——, "Das Mahāyānistische Absolutum nach der Lehre der Mādhyamikas," *Orientalische Literaturzeitung*, XXXVIII (1935), pp. 401-415.

Seng-chao, *Chao-lun* (The Book of Chao), T 1858.

Sengupta, B.K., "A Study of Nāgārjuna," *Indian Historical Quarterly*, XXXI, No. 3 (1955), pp. 257-262.

Sharma, Chandradhar, *Dialectic in Buddhism and Vedānta*. Banaras: Nand Kishore and Brothers, 1952.

Silkstone, Thomas, "My Self and My World," *International Philosophical Quarterly*, 13 (September, 1973), pp. 377-390.

Sogen, Y., *Systems of Buddhistic Thought*. Calcutta: University of Calcutta, 1912.

Sprung, Mervyn (ed.), *The Problem of Two Truths in Buddhism and Vedānta*. Boston: D. Reidel, 1973.

Stcherbatsky, Theodore, *Buddhist Logic*. 2 vols. New York: Dover, 1930.
——, *The Central Conception of Buddhism and the Meaning of the Word Dharma*. Calcutta: Susil Gupta, Ltd., 1956.
——, *The Conception of Buddhist Nirvāṇa*. Leningrad: Publishing Office of the Academy of Sciences of the U.S.S.R., 1927.

Streng, Frederick J., "The Buddhist Doctrine of Two Truths as Religious Philosophy," *Journal of Indian Philosophy*, 1 (November, 1971), pp. 262-271.
——, *Emptiness: A Study in Religious Meaning*. New York: Abingdon, 1967.
——, "Metaphysics, Negative Dialectic, and the Expression of the Inexpressible," *Philosophy East and West*, XXV, No. 4 (October, 1975), pp. 429-447.
——, "On the Attention Given to Mental Construction in the Indian Buddhist Analysis of Causality," *Ibid.*, XXV, No. 1 (January, 1975), pp. 71-80.

Suzuki, Daisetz T., *Essays in Zen Buddhism*. 3rd Series. London: Rider & Company, 1953.
——, *An Introduction to Zen Buddhism*. New York: Grove

Press, 1964.

——, *Outlines of Mahāyāna Buddhism.* New York: Schocken Books, 1963.

——, "Reason and Intuition in Buddhist Philosophy," *Essays in East-West Philosophy* (Charles A. Moore, ed.). Honolulu: University of Hawaii Press, 1951.

——, *Studies in the Laṅkāvatāra Sūtra.* London: Routledge and Kegan Paul Ltd., 1972.

——, *The Laṅkāvatāra Sūtra.* London: Routledge, 1932.

——, *Zen Buddhism.* New York: Doubleday (Anchor Books), 1956.

T'ai-hsu, *T'ai-hsu-ta-shih-ch'uan-shu* (A Collection of Great Master T'ai-hsu's Writings). Vol. 13. Taipei: Great Master T'ai-hsu Committee, 1969.

Taishō Shinshū Daizōkyō (Taishō Edition of the Chinese Tripitaka). Takakusu Junjirō and Watanabe Kaikyoku (eds.), 100 vols. Tokyo: Daizō Shuppan Company, 1924-34.

Takakusu, Jujirō, *The Essentials of Buddhist Philosophy* (W.T. Chan and Charles A. Moore, eds.). Honolulu: University of Hawaii, 1949.

Tanaka, Junshō, "Kūgan no hatten" (The Development of the Doctrine of Emptiness). *Nakano kyōju koki kinen ronbun-shū*; Studies in Indology and Buddhology honoring Prof. Gisho Nakano's 70th Birthday. Kōyasan University: 1960, pp. 83-104.

——, "Kūgan no ronri" (The Logic of Emptiness). *Indogaku Bukkyōgaku Kenkyū*, II, No. 1 (1953), pp. 230-232.

T'ang, Yung-t'ung, *Han-wei Liang-chin Nan-pei-ch'ao Fo-chiao-shih* (History of Buddhism in Han, Wei, the Two Chins and Northern and Southern Dynasties). Shanghai:

Commercial Press, 1938.

Thomas, Edward J., *The History of Buddhist Thought*. London: Routledge & Kegan Paul Ltd., 1933.

Trundle Jr., Robert, "Beyond the Linguistic and Conceptual: A Comparison of Albert Camus and Nāgārjuna," *Darshana International*, XVI (January, 1976), pp. 1-11.

Tsukamoto, Zenryū, ed., *Jōron kenkyū* (Studies in the *Chao-lun*). Kyoto: Hōzōkan, 1960.

Tsunemoto, Kenyū, *Kūgan tetsugaku* (The Philosophy of Emptiness). Tokyo: Daiichi Shobō, 1942.

Tucci, Giuseppe, *Pre-Diṅnāga Buddhist Texts on Logic from Chinese Sources*. Baroda: Oriental Institute, 1929.
——, "Two Hymns of the *Catuḥ-stava* of Nāgārjuna," *Journal of Royal Asiatic Society*, 1932, pp. 309-325.

Ui, Hakuji, "Sanron Kaidai" (The Explanation of Three Treatises), in *Kokuyaku Daizōkyō* (Kyusaka Tsuruda, ed.), Rombu V. Tokyo: Kokumin Bunko Kankō-kai, 1921.
——, *The Vaiśeṣika Philosophy*. London: Royal Asiatic Society, 1917.

Upadhyaya, G., *Buddhism and Hinduism*. Banaras: Banaras Hindu University Publication.

Upadhyaya, Kashi Nath, *Early Buddhism and the Bhagavad-gītā*. Delhi: Motilal Banarsidass, 1971.

Uryūzu, Ryūshin, "Candrakīrti no ātman hihan" (Candra-kīrti's Criticism of *ātman*). *Indogaku Bukkyōgaku Kenkyū*, XI, No. 2 (1963), pp. 344-352.

Vaidya, P.L., *Études sur Āryadeva et son Catuhsataka*. Paris: Geuthner, 1923.

Vidyabhusana, S.C., "History of the Mādhyamika Philosophy of Nāgārjuna," *Journal of the Buddhist Text Society*, 1897, No. 4, pp. 7-20.
——, "The Mādhyamika School," *Ibid.*, 1895, No. 2, pp. 3-9, and No. 3, pp. 9-23.

Waley, Arthur, "New Light on Buddhism in Medieval India," *Mélanges chinois et bouddhiques*, I (1931-32), pp. 335-376.
——, *The Real Tripiṭaka*. London: Allen and Unwin, 1952.
——, "Review of *Jōron Kenkyū*," *Bulletin of the School of Oriental and African Studies*, XIX (London, 1957), pp. 194-196.

Walleser, Max, *Die Mittlere Lehre Nāgārjuna's*. Heidelberg: Carl Winters, Universitätsbuchhandel, 1911 and 1912.
——, "The Life of Nāgārjuna from Tibetan and Chinese Sources," *Asia Major*, Hirth Anniversary vol., pp. 421-455. London: 1922.

Warren, Henry Clarke, *Buddhism in Translation*. New York: Atheneum, 1970.

Wayman, Alex, "Contributions to the Mādhyamika School of Buddhism," *Journal of the American Oriental Society*, Vol. 89, No. 1 (1969), pp. 141-152.

Winternitz, Moriz, *A History of Indian Literature* (S. Ketkar, trans.). University of Calcutta, 1927.

Wong, Mou-lan, ed., *Sūtra Spoken by the Sixth Patriarch on the High Seat of the Treasure of the Law*. Hong Kong: Hong Kong Buddhist Book Distributor Press, 1952.

Yamaguchi, Susumu, "Chūgan Bukkyō ni okeru ushinron no hihan" (The Mādhyamika Critique of Theism), *Bukkyō to Bunka* (Buddhism and Culture), Kyoto, 1960, pp. 68-97.

——, *Chūgwan bukkyō ronkō* (Exploring Mādhyamika Buddhism). Tokyo: Kōbundō Shobō, 1944.

——, "Ejoron ni tsuite" (On the *Vigrahavyāvartanī*), *Mikkyō Bunka*, No. 7 (1949), pp. 1-19; No. 8 (1950), pp. 1-17; No. 9, 10 (1950), pp. 1-20 and No. 12 (1950), pp. 23-31.

——, *Hannya shisō shi* (History of *Prajñā* Thought). Kyoto: Hōzōkan, 1956.

——, "Pour écarter les vaines discussions" (translation of the *Vigrahavyāvartanī*), *Journal Asiatique*, No. 215 (1929), pp. 1-86.

Yamaguchi, Yusuke, *Kū to benshōhō* (Emptiness and Dialectics). Tokyo: Risōsha, 1939.

Yasui, Kōsai, "Chūgan setsu no tachiba to shite no nitai setsu" (Two Truths from the Mādhyamika Perspective), *The Annual Report of Researches of the Otani University*, No. 8 (1955), pp. 59-143.

——, *Chūgan Shisō no Kenkyū* (A Study of Mādhyamika Thought). Kyoto: Hōzōkan, 1961.

——, "Jūnimonron wa hatashite ryūju no chosaku ka?" (Is the *Twelve Gate Treatise* Nāgārjuna's Work?), *Indogaku Bukkyōgaku Kenkyū*, VI, No. 1 (1958), pp. 44-51.

Zōkai, *Jūni monron sho monshi ki* (Notations on the Commentary of the *Twelve Gate Treatise*), T 2257.

Index of Names

203

Index of Subjects